You Are What You Say

You Are What You Say

The Proven Program That
Uses the Power of Language to Combat
Stress, Anger, and Depression

Matthew Budd, M.D., and Larry Rothstein, Ed.D.

Introduction by Patch Adams, M.D.

THREE RIVERS PRESS
NEW YORK

Grateful acknowledgment is made to the following for permission to reprint previously published material: PORTIA NELSON: "Autobiography in Five Chapters" by Portia Nelson. Copyright © 1993 by Portia Nelson, from the book *There's a Hole in My Sidewalk* (Hillsboro, OR: Beyond Words Publishing).

Published by Three Rivers Press, New York, New York. Member of the Crown Publishing Group.

Random House, Inc. New York, Toronto, Sydney, Auckland
www.randomhouse.com

THREE RIVERS PRESS is a registered trademark and the Three Rivers Press colophon is a trademark of Random House, Inc.

Originally published in hardcover by Crown Publishers in 2000.

Printed in the United States of America

Design by Mina Greenstein

Library of Congress Cataloging-in-Publication Data
Budd, Matthew.
You are what you say: the proven program that uses the power of language to combat stress, anger, and depression/Matthew Budd and Larry Rothstein.
Includes bibliographical references and index.
1. Self-talk.   2. Mind and body.   3. Psycholinguistics.   I. Rothstein, Larry.
II. Title.

BF697.5.S47B83   2000
158.1—dc21   99-56084

ISBN 0-8129-2962-4

BVG 01

To

DAVID McCLELLAND,
who had the audacity to study the physiological effects of
unconditional love and the brilliance to anticipate positive
changes

HUMBERTO MATURANA,
who had the strength and courage to base his thinking
about human nature on solid biological evidence even
though the implications clashed with the Western mind

FERNANDO FLORES,
thinker, teacher, and entrepreneur, who had the breadth
to reconcile diverse strands of scholarly and practical
endeavor into a coherent philosophy and the wisdom to
sense the implications of his work for human life

RICHARD HECKLER,
exemplar for the qualities of teachership—expertise,
compassion, generosity, and gentle firmness, "as a robin
holds a worm"

Foreword

Patch Adams, M.D.

WHEN I FIRST HEARD of this book, I had to ask myself, "Is there room for another self-help book on the shelf?" I think not. People already know what they should do . . . they just have trouble breaking old habits and doing it.

But then I read on.

Inspired by the work of Humberto Maturana, the darling of the world of cybernetics, Matt Budd has seen that true learning and change actually involve changing our very structures, our biology. No wonder good advice is not enough.

Maturana has been suggesting that we do not control our language, it controls us. Like other actions—e.g., movement and perception—our language flows from our structure and in turn shapes us. In the book, Matt points out that people can be imprisoned in their language, and he offers us exercises to help us observe and loosen the shackles of our personal confinement.

Matt is both outrageous and generous to take Maturana's difficult concepts and make them seem commonplace. He is quite humble about his efforts and instead of offering "the way" as if he knew it and others didn't, he presents these insights with clarity and simplicity as an offer—an offer that he claims, and backs up with evidence, will support our learning, practice, and health.

His model is that of a "dojo" in which the leader or "sensei" presents material clearly. It falls to the student to first try on, then embody these concepts. In this book he takes the role of sensei; the reader is the student. Practice is essential.

I am delighted that he follows some select types of patients throughout his book to give flesh to his ideas. I see them as theater pieces where over time we see how ideas have effects on people, and how people have effects on ideas, and how the whole system can change for the better.

The difficulty in getting patients to live healthy lives has not been because there has been any lack of clarity for what constitutes healthy living. The difficulty has been in having people put this "good advice" into action. It's hard to get people out of old habits.

Matt, in this book, has dramatically increased this possibility by throwing open the doors to a whole new direction that each one of us can go.

Thank you, Matt.

February 2000

Acknowledgments

THIS BOOK is so autobiographical that I feel obliged to thank everyone who contributed to my life up to this point. This I do in my heart, but in written word it is, of course, impossible.

My principal teachers I have already mentioned in the dedication. My good fortune at having them in my life is a treasure that I can only attribute to luck, a little bit of consciousness on my part, and the gifts of history.

My patients over twenty-eight years of practice have been my everyday mentors. They have continually invited me to sweep aside my internal chatter in their presence. They have asked me to listen to them as human beings in pain, not as diseases to be cured. In my zeal to learn to listen, I was sometimes rough and prying. But always they were faithful and ever-present teachers who inspired me to keep going in my journey to become a doctor and healer.

A number of colleagues showed me that although traditional Western medicine is to be admired and honored, its cognitive blinders need to be lifted. Among these valued pioneers I thank Herbert Benson, David Sobel, Dean Ornish, Redford Williams, and Norman Cousins.

Other colleagues supported, encouraged, and partnered with me. They made traveling an unconventional path less lonely. Among these I include Roberta Colasanti, Margot Fanger, Dick Bail, Carl Isihara, Cathy Vieweg, Catherine O'Brien, Marsha Orlowski, and Jessie Gruman.

Professionals are keepers of the tradition. That's what the certificate on their wall means. As such, many colleagues found what I was doing nontraditional and curious. They forced me to strive for high standards of rigor and validation for my work. This was a great service to me. It's always easier to preach to the converted than to the skeptical. In the act of demonstrating my thinking to the doubters, I was forced to their level of exactness and honesty. My profession contains legions of men and women of the greatest integrity and commitment, and my gratitude to those whom I have worked with is enormous.

I am grateful to Russell Redenbaugh for his personal brilliance and rigor. A phone call to Russell is like a sniff of spirits of ammonia, always clarifying and awakening.

Werner Erhard made accessible to the many wisdom from many sources. His workshops encouraged transformational learning and were a novel innovation. His practical wisdom—encapsulated in phrases like "It's easier to ride the horse in the direction it's going" and "What you resist, persists" and "Understanding is the booby prize"—are with me daily.

Then there is my family. My father, Mark, who believed in me without wavering; my mother, Lillian, who shared every last particle of her wisdom and humor with me; my daughters, Sarah, Karen, Rachel, and Sarah, who each in their way challenged the self that I thought I was; my love and admiration for them kept me "in school" for their lessons.

I blindly decided to write a book. Larry Rothstein knows what a book is—a conversation with a reader. Over countless sessions, he has forced me to listen rather than to write, to be a teacher rather than a lecturer, to be open rather than to be smart. Larry, thank you for your brilliance and your patience.

I wish also to acknowledge Wendy Lynch of Mercer-Meinenger, a fellow traveler in the understanding of mind-body medicine. Wendy gave me invaluable assistance in the development of the self-assessment tool contained in this book.

In addition, I want to thank Betsy Rapoport, my editor at Crown books, and Kristine Dahl, my agent at International Creative Management, for their guidance and encouragement throughout this process.

And finally my thanks to my beloved wife, Roz. My mission is her mission because she says so. What a gift!

MATTHEW BUDD, M.D., *February 2000*

Contents

You Are What You Say

Life as an Awakening Place

The best way to make your dreams come true is to wake up.
— Paul Valéry

Insanity is doing the same thing over and over hoping that it will turn out differently.
— Rita Mae Brown

Are you having problems with your health, your vitality and energy? Do you have one or more of the chronic conditions that I see every day as a doctor, such as severe headaches, jaw and neck problems, insomnia, stomach and bowel problems, depression, lack of energy, and high blood pressure? Does your life seem more like a struggle than a work of art?

If this is so, ask yourself: What is happening in my life that is causing me to suffer and not feel well? Do you have serious problems at home or at work? Are you overwhelmed because you can't say no to those around you? Do your children drive you crazy? Do you feel that you never have enough money? Do you distrust others? Do you feel unloved and joyless most of the time? Are you often embarrassed, isolated, or upset?

Can you see yourself yet on this human menu? Can you start to observe that there is a connection between how you live and feel in your life and your state of health?

Now ask yourself this: Do I want to change these circumstances? Do I want to learn how to live a different life, one filled with health, joy, and happiness?

If the answers are yes, then this book is for you.

But be prepared for surprises. This book is unlike any self-help book you've ever read. It describes a program that is a unique synthesis of ancient wisdom and new insights into health and healing. It builds on medicine's recent breakthroughs regarding the mind-body connection, but moves dramatically beyond them to help you learn how literally to create a new mind and build a new body. And it does this through a few simple exercises that involve acknowledging the impact your personal history has had on your life, learning how your practices in language affect and reflect who you are and how you can use language in a healthier way, gaining control of your moods and emotions and becoming aware of the automatic thoughts that play like a jukebox in your head.

The Ways to Wellness Program

Thousands of people just like you have been participating in this kind of learning for nearly twenty years at the Harvard Community Health Plan (HCHP), a Harvard Medical School–affiliated health maintenance organization located in Boston.

In 1982, my colleagues and I at HCHP made our first attempts to synthesize what we were learning about mind-body medicine into a program for patients with emotional and physical stress. Two colleagues, Margot Fanger and Roberta Colasanti, and I named our course "Ways to Wellness." As we observed the progress that our patients made in the course, my colleagues and I were ecstatic—their accomplishments exceeded our predictions. It was as if the work of the course had released a passion for healing that had previously been unavailable to them. Patients accomplished in a few short weeks what we had been unable to do for them for years through explanation and medication. We weren't fixing these people, they were healing themselves. We were acting as facilitators.

The Ways to Wellness program is a six-week educational course with home exercises between each session. Primary care physicians refer a majority of the patients to the program; other patients take the course on the advice of a friend or family member. A version of the program, the Personal Health Improvement Program (PHIP), is now taught by HMOs and health programs in seventeen states.

Some patients who come to the course have a specific disease they are struggling with, such as high blood pressure or heart problems. Other patients have symptoms of a chronic nature for which no cause can be found, such as headaches or anxiety attacks. Still others want more out of life and know that they themselves are somehow getting in the way of their own health.

Scientific studies of the Ways to Wellness course show that our patients achieve valuable and sustained improvement in their emotional lives, their physical well-being, and their daily functioning. In their emotional lives, they are less anxious and depressed and more trusting. Patients who participate in this course also have fewer physical complaints. Some take fewer medications or stop taking medicines completely. (Of course, they make decisions about medication in consultation with their physician.) And the quality of our patients' lives improves dramatically—they tell us they have more satisfaction, more vitality, a better time with friends, and so on.

For example, Carol, a forty-three-year-old architect, was constantly angry with her children, her husband, and with herself. She was plagued by anxiety attacks that would send her fleeing to hospital emergency rooms because she feared she was having a heart attack. Although the tests always proved negative, Carol couldn't rid herself of the fear that she would soon die.

In the Ways to Wellness program, Carol began to observe her automatic reactions of fear and anger and the impact they were having on her health. As she performed the course's exercises and developed awareness of her habits, Carol's way of seeing things changed—she, in essence, was creating a new mind—and as her emotional reaction to situations altered, she began building a new body. Carol began to experience more joy with her family and from her work. The anxiety attacks became less intense and their frequency declined. After a while they stopped. Now, when Carol feels pressure from her husband, her family, or from work, she sees it earlier and more clearly, she recognizes its source, and she takes appropriate action, rather than exploding in anger.

John, a thirty-eight-year-old entrepreneur, came to the program with severe stomach problems. During the course, he learned to face the truth about what was causing his problem. He had made several bad business investments that had led him to lose a million dollars; John began to realize that for years he had brutally blamed himself and others for his reverses. Through the course he saw the futility of living in a regretful past, and began to work off his debts. As he took control of his life and became less of a victim, his health improved, most notably his stomach problems.

Betty, a fifty-one-year-old real estate broker, was hypercritical of herself and everyone around her. The result is that she was always frustrated and alone. She came to the program suffering from chronic pelvic pain, a common lower abdominal complaint of women. As she did the work of the course, Betty's pain lessened and she began a romantic relationship with a fellow real estate agent.

These are not miracle cures but the fruits of committed learning. As you will see in this book, improvements in your daily functioning, your emotional life, and your health tend to occur together, as a unity. When things in life work for you, your emotions and health improve.

I Am a Beginner

The path of learning that led to this book began when I admitted to myself that I was miserable and frustrated. Shortly after I finished my medical training and entered practice, I discovered that I could not help many of my patients. It's not that I hadn't learned my medical lessons well. The truth was that I was an excellent student and a competent physician. The problem was with what I was taught, or more accurately what I *wasn't* taught.

I was highly competent in treating disease, but couldn't help people who were suffering in various and very common ways like the people I mentioned above. Finally, in desperation, I admitted this to myself: I was not as effective as I could be and it bothered me a lot.

As a consequence of acknowledging this truth, I declared myself a beginner in the human aspects of care. This led me to search for new teachers, new insights, and new practices. It also led me to study psychology, philosophy, biology, neurobiology, and religious thinking, both Western and Eastern. As I opened a new path of learning and action for myself, I found joy and fulfillment, as well as new problems and questions. That's the way life is. When we take responsibility for our suffering, new possibilities emerge.

Over the years, I've refined what I learned into the core set of principles and practices of this program. The weaving of old wisdom with the new and the scientific makes up the heart of this book and accounts for the power of this program.

A Learning Space

One of the keys of the Ways to Wellness program is that it creates what I call a *learning space.*

People learn in several distinct ways. One way I call *informational* or *instructional learning.* A teacher or a book tells you the facts or procedures about something—what to believe and what to do—and you do what you will with the information. If I read a travel article about Trinidad, I learn about beaches, restaurants, and available water sports. But after I do, I'm still the same person that I was before reading the article. This is a one-size-fits-all kind of learning. In this kind of learning, the instructions dominate; who the learner is is almost irrelevant.

A second kind of learning involves *apprenticeship.* In this kind of learning, you find someone who is a master, a silversmith like Paul Revere. You make a commitment to learn, and your mentor makes a commitment to teach. You watch and learn by watching. From time to time, Paul allows you to do a more advanced task. After a while, when he thinks you're ready, you make your first silver bowl. Paul then examines the bowl and coaches you on how to make an even better bowl.

This time-honored approach to learning always involves a master, it takes a lot of time, and most important, the objects you initially turn out generally look like the master's—better or, more likely, worse copies. Your learning is very much tied to the style of the master. Your personal creativity and uniqueness are secondary.

A third kind of learning is *self-help learning.* This method is characterized by tips and techniques on how to do things better. Stephen Covey's *The Seven Habits of Highly Effective People* is an example of this kind of learning. Tips and techniques orient you to kinds of actions and principles of effectiveness. The advice also tends to be concise and pithy—not a lot to learn and quick, "fast-food" learning. This learning is very consistent with American values and culture.

The problem with this kind of learning is execution. These books focus on outcomes but don't provide a lot of advice on how to achieve those outcomes.

This book will encourage an entirely different kind of learning from those described above, what I call *embodied learning.* This kind of learning entails discovering how you routinely and automatically behave in a given situation. Then, using new distinctions and practices, you will learn to change your capacity to act.

Embodied learning involves learning to act in living. You are on the field as a player, not on the sidelines as a coach, or in the stands as a spectator, or in the press box as a reporter. You *are* the show. The ball is heading for you. Catch it, or not—but don't just stand there and watch it or talk about it.

Simple to understand, but far from easy to achieve. As you shall see, old habits are hard to change because they have the force of biological inertia behind them. Every time I walk past a bowl of chocolates, my hand automatically reaches out to take one or two. We are all like that in other areas. My remembering, or someone reminding me, that too much chocolate is bad for me won't stop me. Sustainable change takes awareness of what's driving the behavior, but, more importantly, new practices for changing the behavior and a belief that change is possible.

Don't worry about understanding exactly what I'm saying at this point. Focus on this pattern of learning: awareness, new concepts, practice, and coaching. This is the pattern of this book. It parallels many of the features of what in the martial arts is called a dojo, except this is a dojo for health.

The Spirit of the Dojo

Dojo literally means "an awakening place." The term *dojo* generally refers to a martial arts learning center in which participants are urged to "wake up" to the unconscious tendencies that interfere with their martial arts performance. In our dojo of health, we'll focus on transforming destructive habits that interfere with satisfying life performance and hence jeopardize health.

In this dojo, I am the sensei, meaning I have embodied some of the distinctions in the past and at least have the competence to show them to you. I've been a sensei for eighteen years as a teacher, physician, and leader. My only claim for myself is that I've been a beginner who has practiced and is on a learning path. I continue to have my own sensei out of my commitment to my own lifelong learning.

In this dojo you are the student. Are you willing to be a student? Are you willing to not know? Are you willing to be confused at times for the sake of later clarity? Are you willing to strive for precision in your observations about yourself? Are you willing to make mistakes? (All beginners do.) Are you willing to practice? If you can honestly say yes to these questions, I invite you to be a beginner.

A dojo is built on a family of precise distinctions. By "distinction" I mean words that point to specific ways of acting or seeing. "Keep your weight on the downhill ski" is a phrase a ski instructor might utter. "Downhill ski" is a useful *distinction* in skiing. In the martial arts the key distinctions are certain moves, defenses, attacks, and the like. These distinctions have been shown over time to be valid. In the dojo, students go into action with the distinctions given to them by the sensei and do their routines. The sensei then guides the students in the observation of themselves in action. Seeing oneself is sometimes very difficult, but this method allows a student to see himself or herself through the eyes of the sensei, and then to try the practice again, making corrections. At some point, the student begins to embody more and more of the sensei's critical eye and avoid errors. After a while, he or she is ready to be a sensei to others. This cycle of listening, acting, observing, changing, and acting again is the process of the dojo—the process of building embodied learning.

This is what will happen in our health dojo. In this kind of environment I have experienced deep personal learning. I began to see, for example, that I used the authority of being a doctor to shore up and defend against personal self-doubts. Facing the truth was not easy, but once I did, personal doubt had less of a grip on me, and I became a more self-confident doctor.

What about you? Are you willing to face the truth regardless of the emotion it evokes? Or do you prefer to continue in a tranquilized numbness? We all have areas in life in which we are numb, but once we commit to shining light on those areas we are beginners. Are you ready to be a beginner?

The Book

This book's structure and content parallel what we teach in the Ways to Wellness course and the Personal Health Improvement program. The book is divided into two parts that present the core concepts that I learned in roughly the same chronological order that I learned them. I chose this autobiographical format because the program is one of lived learning. I test the validity of this learning by using it every day in my life when I encounter problems. Until I learned these principles and practices, or at least began the lifelong process of learning by living, I didn't know their power and couldn't invite others to join with me on this journey. "Walking the talk" is always a critical challenge. Each chapter is followed by an exercise section that will assist you in bringing the distinctions into your life.

In chapter 1, "My Black Bag Is Half Empty," I describe an event that I witnessed at a New Age training session that radically changed my understanding of mind-body relationships. I also discuss my medical training, the frustration that I felt when I found that such knowledge couldn't help many of my patients, and how a remembered childhood experience with my grandmother made sense for the first time.

Also in this chapter, you will meet four patients who are typical of the kind of people who participate in this course. Their problems, their approach to learning, their struggles with learning are likely to be similar to yours. You may identify with one of them, and this person will be a kind of guide as you go through the book. Or you may identify with certain aspects of each of them. For example, you may identify with Walter's anger and find yourself falling into anger as you begin these exercises. Or you may identify with Linda's low self-esteem and share some of her experiences as you learn. Her insights may prove valuable, even inspiring to you.

These people are real people. Their names and some details have been changed to hide their identity.

Chapter 2, "We Are Animals, but We Have Forgotten," reminds you that you are a biological being. Your knowledge and ability to know things must follow biological principles. You can only be and do what your body allows.

In chapter 3, "History, the Sculptor of Our Being," I show how individual experience and cultural history shape your identity as a person, including your reactions, emotions, actions, etc. You'll see that there are no accidents in life—at every moment you do what you can do. You can act in no other way.

I introduce you to a new understanding of language in chapter 4, "You Are What You Say." Most people believe that language describes reality. I argue that language brings forth reality. You know the expression "You are what you eat." Well, I claim, "You are what you say."

In chapter 5, "Reasons of the Heart," I look at moods and emotions. Here I emphasize that moods occur in the body and alter not only bodily function and perception, but also affect health and daily activity.

Most of my patients think they are powerless over their moods. This is not so. By the end of the book, you'll see how to interact with your moods in a highly constructive way.

In chapter 6, "Putting It All Together," I describe the integration of the elements that you have been learning about your body, mind, history, language, and mood into a program of lifelong education. In addition, I remind you of the importance of self-awareness, which is essential for personal learning and transformation, and I examine several practices for cultivating this valuable skill.

I hope you'll find the material in these explanatory chapters thought-provoking, and that it will encourage self-examination and questioning. But most people probably read as observers, standing outside looking in, without much personal involvement. You learn *about* something rather than learning it experientially.

By "learn about," I mean that kind of learning that's like watching a movie. In that situation, you're a spectator—you don't get shot at, or catch the good-looking lover, or defeat the aliens. You watch other people act, and you experience these events vicariously. You may be amused, frightened, or angered, but you are at a safe distance. This is a useful kind of experience, one that entertainment is all about. But there is much more available to you from this book.

Now it's time for you to make a decision. Are you content simply to learn *about* this program, or are you going to learn by *living* it? Are you willing to be the lead actor in this movie about living life peacefully and in good health? I can give you a script, I can even help to direct you in a general way, but you must play the part fully and convincingly. You must win your own Oscar. The reward for this level of engagement is lifelong learning.

Lifelong Learning

What then is lifelong learning? The kind of learning this book provides you with has no end. When life serves up the next challenge to you—a divorce, a business failure, the death of a parent or spouse, a child who's behaving badly, illness, or death—you can either learn or you can suffer with the same behaviors that haven't worked for a long time, if ever.

The pianist Artur Rubinstein once said that each time he played a great piece of music such as a Beethoven sonata, he learned something new. This master was open to lifelong learning. Even though the critics acclaimed each performance, he was never satisfied. Rubinstein was always searching for a new way to play.

Your life can be the same way. Each time you return to the sonata of your life with intention and attention, you'll see something new. You may ignore what you see—people often do; everything has its time. Or you may observe how an old narrative of fear twists your current behavior. Or you may make a declaration to change something. The choice is yours.

The aim of your journey could be the experience and expression of love, clarity, and freedom, not a specifically defined destination, goal, or reward. This is not a popular modern notion. For most of us, getting something or somewhere is the name of the game. Remember the bumper sticker "He who dies with the most toys wins"? That is a game of greed, of uneasiness, of fear. Will I win? Do I have enough? Will I live a long time? Will my children succeed? There is nothing intrinsically wrong with these questions, but they provoke anxiety, uneasiness, and fear in me. Do they do the same for you?

This book is not about that game. Its goal is to help you manifest your natural capacity for learning and satisfaction with your life, for love, compassion, and wellness.

The "I Am the Way I Am" Syndrome

A major enemy of lifelong learning is living in the interpretation that "I am the way I am and I can't change." Versions of this include: "I'm too stupid," "I don't trust any teachers," and "I know already." These statements are ones of low self-efficacy, distrust, and arrogance. They are expressions of deep fears, the shards of past hurts. They reveal a person at risk for suffering and even illness.

More importantly, these attitudes inhibit learning and blind you from the realization that you are their author. As the famous physicist David Bohm pointed out, your system of thought hides itself as the author of what you see, think, and do. When you fall into distrust, arrogance, or self-denigration, you believe you are describing reality. But you're not. Your thoughts generate a closed mind, an inflexible person, a victim, not a warrior.

How then do you deal with your system of thought? For some people, learning only occurs when they have "hit bottom." For each of us, there have been moments when our incompetence was so evident, when blaming others for our pain was so blatantly hollow, when our excuses and justifications were so exhausted that we had to admit our responsibility for our own suffering. When that happens, we then may decide to do something about our lives. Crisis may breed a kind of forced "openness."

But this is an expensive way of learning—wasteful of life and costly in terms of suffering. If you are wise, there are easier ways of ending the "I am the way I am" syndrome.

For example, you can be inspired by someone's skillful handling of situations that are similar to yours. Another motivation for change can come when you realize you have the potential for learning and action. You may begin to question the self-imposed barriers that limit your growth. You might ask, "Could I be my own worst enemy?" When you do this, you open yourself to learning.

Escape from the "I am the way I am" syndrome also happens when someone you trust encourages you to learn. A good coach does this. Or a friend, or loved one. Sometimes even a child. He or she knows you can do better than you are doing now, even though you may not even see this or understand how this could happen. The real issue is trust. Can you suspend judgment and trust a teacher long enough to learn?

I'm reminded of the story of Alice, a young piano prodigy. After enrolling at a prestigious Boston conservatory for lessons with a master teacher, Alice couldn't wait to start playing for him. Instead, the master teacher went to the piano and played a progression of ten notes. He then asked Alice to play them back just as he did. When Alice finished, he said, "You must learn to listen if you are to be a serious performer. Repeat the ten notes exactly as I played them." With that he repeated the exercise. They continued this way for the entire first lesson.

During the next six months, before Alice was allowed to play the compositions that she had prepared, she and the master teacher would spend a large part of their hour on this exercise. Finally, after six months of Alice's frustrated questioning ("Why do I have to do this?"), impatience, and even anger, the master teacher finally exclaimed, "That's it, you got it. Now you are listening! Now you can learn to play."

I know you have the capacity to learn. I have faith in your capacity to change. Nature, or God, didn't create you to suffer. I can't make you play the ten notes, but I say that if you do the exercises in this book, you will learn. I can say this because I know that biologically your structure is plastic—i.e., capable of change. Whatever your age, sex, background, or educational level, this biological truth holds. I've seen students in an assisted living home, with an average age of eighty-eight, learn.

In this book, I'm your coach. I've been coach to several thousands of people like you. I assume this role based on my background as a physician, biologist, and teacher. Because of my experience, I believe that your most troublesome areas of life are where the most learning will occur. To do this, you'll need to make clear distinctions, become aware of your current tendencies, design new behaviors, and practice. In short, you need to become a beginner.

For most of us, being a beginner is to be avoided at all cost. We need to look good, to be in control, to appear to have all the answers all of the time. But this is not a universal aspiration. In fact, Buddhists strive for what they call "beginner's mind," the mind of not knowing. Such not knowing is not blindness or ignorance. Rather, it involves the state of being present to what is, not to your story about what is.

Exercises: Design and Content

I encourage you to read a chapter, then do the exercises relevant to it. This will help you move from passive observer to active participant. The exercises that follow each explanatory chapter will help you achieve beginner's mind and open yourself to learning. When you begin to do the exercises, you'll automatically have conversations with yourself such as: "I already know this," "This is crazy," "I can't do this." When this happens, shift your intention and attention away from this internal conversation by continuing to practice the exercises. As you do, try to see what you see.

With practice, you'll become more competent at generating a mind of freshness and presence, not the boring mind of repetition and history. Beginner's mind will become more available to you.

You may not fully understand the workbook exercises, or why you are doing them. Don't worry. Just do them.

I suggest that you spend several days practicing the exercises in each chapter. Do as many of them as you can, given the other events in your life. Pace yourself. You need time to learn, observe, and practice. If you rush, you'll be feeding your mind, not changing your body. If you bog down doing any of the exercises, recommit to your desire to learn. Then try again. Speed is not important.

After each of the exercises or questions, I've left spaces for you to take notes or jot down reminders about what the exercise triggered for you. In many places, you'll probably want to do more extensive writing, so please use a journal or keep a computer file.

For me, writing makes me be more specific and rigorous about what I'm saying. When I think something, I can leave the details fuzzy and keep my distance from them. But when I have to write something for another person to read, I become more precise and involved. My attention and intention to communicate increase. I get clearer. In the end, writing helps me as much as it does the reader.

This has been my experience in writing this book—I've achieved a clearer and deeper sense of what this material is about. So I recommend that you use the writing exercises to deepen and accelerate your learning. When you're finished writing, read and reread what you've written and listen deeply to the voice that you hear. You will discover a treasure.

Another thing that I've learned is to return after a day or two to what I wrote and modify or add to it. You'll experience new things, new outlooks between each writing. One woman who used this book says that she returns to certain exercises weekly, to go deeper into them.

Finally, I'll share with you what I and my patients Gretchen, Walter, Robert, and Linda learned as we did these exercises. Let yourself be inspired by their and my learning. Allow us to clarify concerns you have about the exercises.

If you find yourself comparing your progress to theirs in some competitive or embarrassed way, notice that. Does this kind of comparing go on in your daily life? Begin to observe that. You will learn at *your* speed in *your* way. This is the right way for you, as our path was the right way for us.

Keys to Happiness

There is a Sufi story about an old man who as he passed a streetlight saw a neighbor on his hands and knees. "What are you doing, my friend?" the old man asked.

"I'm looking for my keys," the neighbor said.

"Oh," the old man responded, "I'll help you find them. Where did you lose them?"

"Over there by my house," the neighbor replied.

"Then why are you looking for them under the street lamp?" the old man queried.

"Because this is where the light is!" said the neighbor.

This inability to look in the right place is the reason most of us struggle in life. Our intentions are good, but we repeat old, destructive patterns because that's where we believe the light is. We never question the assumptions that lead us away from discovering the keys to our happiness.

The exercises will help you find the missing keys to your happiness. They will help you create a new mind and build a new body. But the responsibility for doing the exercises remains with you.

Bardos

In Eastern philosophy, there exists the notion of the *bardo*. A bardo is a sticking place, a problem area. It is a moment in life when you can no longer tolerate what is happening around you. Your blame of others, your old explanations of why you have problems in your life lead you nowhere. Even you are tired of your excuses—the suffering is simply too great.

You may even hit several bardos in the course of doing this program. You may think, "This is silly stuff," or "I don't have the time to do this," or "It won't work." Another common one is "I already know all this." These are some of the things you may say to yourself; your reaction to the bardo that the book has created.

The question is not will this occur, but what will you do with this reaction, which hides uncertainty and fear? Will you deny it and blame others? Will you seethe with anger? Will you fall into despair that life will never be good again? Or will you accept that you have encountered yourself in another bardo, and that you are at a moment of choice—a choice between letting go of old static explanations and committing to learning, or believing your old explanations and quitting. If you choose the latter, and sometimes we all do, then what you'll get is more of the same—some degree of suffering and "being right." If you choose to suspend your reaction and learn, then you'll have the possibility of the book truly being an awakening place, your own personal dojo.

It's my intention in writing this book to join my voice, with humility, with the chorus of teachers before me and around me who have chosen the possibility that life can be an awakening place. I invite you to do the same.

My Black Bag Is Half Empty

One spring morning nearly twenty years ago, as I sat in a hotel meeting room with two hundred other participants attending a weekend-long workshop on "personal transformation," I thought I had made one of the biggest mistakes of my life. Yet within a few minutes, I saw something that threatened the scientific underpinnings of everything I understood as a doctor.

Here's what happened. For nearly ten minutes, Irving, the session trainer, had been barking out what he called "the ground rules." A short, stocky man with a balding head and a thunderous voice, Irving had been rattling off a list of things participants were not allowed to do during the training—no eating or drinking in the room, no bathroom breaks except every two hours, no talking to other people in the seminar, and so on.

As Irving droned—or I should say roared—on, all I could think about was that my weekend was ruined. I had questioned the wisdom of my attending this "course" even before I had arrived. After all, I was a Harvard Medical School professor, an internist at one of the country's leading HMOs, and, at the very least, a rational person. So why was I sitting here prepared to listen to ideas that my colleagues at Harvard would and did dismiss with derisive laughter?

The answer was simple—I was in despair. I believed I was an ineffective doctor, unable to help the majority of my patients with their everyday health problems, which were, to my then naïve understanding, largely stress-related or "psychosomatic." Whatever I did for or to them, e.g., mood pills or pain relievers, changed little in their lives. I had become so upset about my inability to help these many patients that I was even considering becoming a surgeon, a doctor who "really helped" people.

I had almost reached this decision when I had lunch with my old friend, a hospital administrator named Shu-Shu. I was complaining to her about my unhappiness when she looked up from her Caesar salad and said, "Why don't you take the training course called est that I've just completed. I think it'll help." I had heard some stories about this training and had an arrogant negative opinion of it. It was reputed to be authoritarian, confrontational, the invention of an encyclopedia salesman. I thought, "How could Shu-Shu be taken in by such a charlatan?"

I replied, "I don't need advice from a bunch of whackos. How can this help me?"

"Trust me," Shu-Shu said, as she waved her salad fork at me. "You'll see, it's really good." I was conflicted. Over the years I'd known her, I had come to admire and respect her deeply. She was a solid, effective person. It was a measure of my desperation that I decided to trust her and to sign up for the weekend course.

My initial instincts seemed correct as Irving continued on with his list of don'ts. I checked my watch—8:10 A.M. The day had just begun, and already it seemed interminable. Irving read the next ground rule, which was "No watches or timepieces." I scowled as I surrendered my watch, placing it into a large box with dozens of others.

I reminded myself never to listen to even good friends' advice. But within minutes, Shu-Shu's promise to me came true.

I noticed a woman seated across the aisle from me. She was coughing uncontrollably. I caught sight of her name tag, which read "Barbara." She was an attractive woman in her late twenties. She wore blue jeans, a white T-shirt, and the platform shoes so popular in that era. Her long, red hair fell lazily halfway down her back.

Suddenly, Barbara's coughing increased in intensity. She began wheezing. I realized that she was having an asthma attack. Asthma is a condition in which the air passages go into spasm and a person's breathing becomes difficult. An asthma attack can be really serious, even fatal. Barbara's breathing now sounded like air whistling out of a balloon with a pinhole in it.

I started out of my seat to see if I could help her. My mind was racing through possible causes for the attack: "Maybe she ate something for breakfast that she was allergic to, or maybe it's the paint or rugs in this hall, or maybe there's a fungus in the air-conditioning system."

But before I could get to Barbara, she jumped out of her seat to challenge one of Irving's ground rules—the one that insisted that participants raise their hand and wait to be called on before speaking. She was barely able to utter her protest—"Don't tell me what to do"—before she was racked by another coughing fit. Irving started walking toward Barbara. At the same time, as I reached her side, I shouted out, "This woman is having an asthma attack." Irving waved me away. He stopped right in front of Barbara and said, "Did you hear the ground rules? No talking until you're called on! I didn't call on you."

Another spasm of coughing ripped through Barbara's body. She doubled up in pain. Irving crouched down until he was two feet from her face. He stared directly into her eyes and said firmly but compassionately, "Look at me, I am not your father!" When I heard this, I was sure that he was crazy.

Barbara grew angrier at these words. Her breathing became even more labored. My anger rose also and I was about to demand that Irving back off so I could attend to Barbara when he said, "Barbara, look at my right ear." The odd nature of Irving's request focused Barbara for a moment. She stared at Irving's right ear. Irving held his gaze on Barbara as he asked, "It's not your father's ear, is it?" She wheezed, "No, of course not." Then Irving repeated his question for his nose, eyes, mouth, and head. Each time, Barbara responded with an irritated no.

Then Irving said, "I'm not your father, am I? So why are you so angry? Just raise your hand and wait to be called on before you speak," he said softly and compassionately.

I couldn't believe what I saw over the next few minutes. Barbara began to cry, a whole body cry, not a polite sob. Looking up from her sadness, she said, "No, you're not my father, but it feels that way." Even as she made this remark, her wheezing lessened and her body visibly relaxed. After a couple of minutes, she was breathing normally and sobbing bitterly.

Now it was me who was gasping. I had seen something that completely upset my worldview. I believed that asthma is a disease caused by the body's response to a substance to which it is allergic. Every first-year medical student knows this. If someone had described what had happened to Barbara, I would have been amused and very skeptical. But I didn't hear or read about it, *I had seen it with my own eyes.* Her attack had cleared up without the aid of inhaled or intravenous medications, the usual treatments for asthma. Irving's questions and Barbara's responses had done the trick. This was incomprehensible to me given everything that I had learned and understood as a doctor about disease, allergy, and treatment.

In fact, as Barbara proclaimed that Irving was not her father and began to cry, I watched her whole body change. The tension and fear left her face, her shoulders lowered from their tightened position, and her breath came more easily.

My brain was spinning with questions. What had happened? What had I been missing as I tried to help my patients? What did Irving know that I didn't? What has modern medicine been missing? How could Irving's words change Barbara's body?

As I sat there in a confused state in the hotel meeting room, I noticed that my despair about medical practice was lifting. I had a whole new set of questions that would stay with me continually during the years that followed. It was clear to me at that moment that engaging these questions would be my life's work.

My Certain World

What happened to Barbara didn't fit my picture of asthma and its treatments. I, like every person, live in a world that looks certain—I know what I know and what I don't know. For example, I know that oxygen is necessary for human life, but I don't know how to fly an airplane.

This certainty is not only true of external things, but extends to our knowledge of ourselves. We know who we are, what is possible and what is not, what we fear and what we welcome. "Public speaking is very difficult," we might say. We say it like a truth, but obviously, public speaking isn't difficult for some people like Bill Clinton or Oprah Winfrey.

Living in a network of "truths" about how things are and are not can be dangerous to your health if you never question the source of these "truths" and ask how it is that you know them.

The most obvious source of "truth" comes from our culture. When we live in the culture, we are not always aware of the cultural nature of these truths. They become our common sense. Nonetheless, they determine the shape of our lives. Interaction with someone of another culture who lives in other "truths" propels us into this awareness.

Consider the following statements. In the background of each one there is a set of assumptions about how things are, the "truths" that determine what is possible and what is not.

"The earth is flat, so of course we might fall off if we sail far enough."
"Her cattle died, so of course she must be a witch."

"He has a fever, which means he has too much blood. To cure him, we
must drain his body of excess blood."

Each of these utterances could have been made by a perfectly rational human being given the understandings of his or her times. For instance, the statement "The earth is flat, so of course we might fall off if
we sail far enough" made sense until Columbus's voyage. In light of the
assumption of flatness, it was perfectly rational that the earth had an
edge that one could fall off of. Of course, no one ever saw the edge. But
proof of its existence was derived from the fact that many seamen in
those days who set sail never returned to port. Therefore, they must have
fallen off the edge!

After Columbus's voyage, the old assumption of flatness appeared
nonsensical, and gradually its hold on people's behavior lessened. The
old common sense died; a new common sense developed.

The statement "Her cattle died, so of course she must be a witch"
was perfectly reasonable for people who inhabited the Western world in
the sixteenth century. They believed the devil could invade the body of a
human, usually a woman. A woman so possessed became a witch. Such
events as the death of cattle or someone falling ill were explained by the
witch's nearby presence.

The remedy was for the time perfectly reasonable—ritual burning of
the witch, thereby saving both her and her community from the devil's
destructive power.

Another example: "He has a fever, which means he has too much
blood. To cure him, we must drain his body of excess blood"—hence,
blood-letting was an approved treatment during the Middle Ages. At
that time, the theories of Galen, the great second century physician,
dominated medical practice. He had hypothesized that normal health resulted from the balance of the body's four "humors"—blood, phlegm,
black bile, and yellow bile. According to Galen, an illness with fever occurred when there was too much blood in the body. So, of course, blood-
letting made sense. The rationale was impeccable, the assumptions
accepted without further examination, the proof was the occasional recovery of a patient. A doctor's training included knowing how many
blood-sucking leeches, of what kind, and how long to apply to a patient.

This kind of mistaken understanding of the world is easy to point out
if we look at the past. But it is much harder to see in our own lives in the
present. Most of us never question how we *know* what we know. One of
this book's goals is to help you uncover your "common sense"—those as-

sumptions about yourself, about others, and about life in general that shape you but remain unexamined.

Here are some of the "truths" that people live with:

- □ Men can't be trusted.
- □ I must strive for perfection.
- □ I can't learn as easily as others can.
- □ People are dangerous.
- □ My life is hopeless and no one can help me.
- □ Everyone is better than me.

(What are your truths? Even though we're early in our journey, begin now to ask yourself that question.)

From that moment nearly twenty years ago when Barbara and Irving opened a door for me through which I could glimpse a new way of treating my patients, I have been involved in a journey toward a new understanding. As part of this journey I began to reflect on my own life and ask how I came to see things the way I did. Over time, I realized that there were important events and people in my life that had shaped my values and beliefs, but I was only dimly aware of them at the time. Later, with additional learning and reflection, I saw these experiences with greater clarity.

One such event involved my grandmother Minnie.

Minnie's Wisdom

One day when I was ten years old, I arrived home early from school. I felt feverish and achy. I headed directly for the comfort of my bedroom. My grandmother Minnie, who had come to live in our house after the death of her husband, Jake, followed me upstairs and asked, "What's wrong?"

Minnie was a short, keenly alert, thick-waisted woman of Eastern European origin, who like hundreds of thousands of other Jews had fled political persecution for a better life in America. Minnie's education was limited; she could neither read nor write English, and before she married she had been a sweatshop laborer. But she was wise, rich in the wisdom of life. Her wisdom came from having observed life and learned well the folk practices of her shtetl.

As I plunked myself down on my bed without replying to her, Minnie asked again, "What's wrong?"

I pulled the covers over my head and said, "I'm sick." But Minnie would not let things lie. Like an impassioned scientist on the trail of a new discovery, she persisted: "Why are you sick? You were okay this morning."

I still remember the irritation that question provoked in me. I wanted her to leave me alone. Sensing my ire, Minnie told me she'd brew up a batch of chicken soup, her all-purpose remedy for illness. But as she left the room she advised, "Think about my question. Why are you sick?"

As the minutes passed, the day's events flooded my mind.

I *was* well when I left for school, baseball glove and books tucked under my arm. In fact, I was well until recess, when the boys in my class decided to play a pickup game of baseball. "Stinky" DelMonte, the class bully, was my team's self-appointed captain. He assigned me to play right field. Right field? That's where baseball misfits were exiled! I always played shortstop. I pleaded my case to Stinky, but he only shouted, "I'm in charge here. Right field or nothing."

I was furious, embarrassed, and afraid at the same time. Stinky towered over me. I knew he could beat me up if I challenged him. Head down, I sulked toward right field. With each step I took, I felt worse. After one inning I left the game and went to the school nurse. "It looks like flu" was her diagnosis, and she sent me home.

As my replay of events ended, Minnie returned to the room with a piping-hot bowl of chicken soup. "Here, eat this and you'll feel better," she said. And in the next breath asked that question again: "Why are you sick?"

As I sipped the soup, I blurted out the story of the pickup game. I talked about my deep disappointment, but more important, my helplessness in the face of the bully. As I look back now at that event, the bully had challenged my "truth" about myself as a baseball player. By force he compelled me to play in a way that was inconsistent with my beliefs about myself. I was hurt and angry. Tears streamed down my cheeks.

"I know how bad you feel," Minnie said. "I too have known bullies." Today, I realize that she must have been thinking of the Cossack pogroms that terrified her peaceful little village in Poland. She gave me no more advice, just her compassionate presence and attention.

Somehow after I told my story I began to feel better, more relaxed. No miracle cures, but I fell asleep. When I awoke four hours later, I felt almost well enough to play baseball.

This experience remained locked away in my memory like a buried treasure until decades later, when I began to understand in a scientific way what Minnie had known instinctively—that the mind and the body are part of the same unity, and one affects the other. Moreover, Minnie showed me the cornerstone of helping someone who was suffering—just listen.

I Want to Be a Doctor

On a crisp, crystal-clear fall afternoon nearly ten years later, I was seated on the fifty-yard line during the traditional Amherst-Williams football game. I was a sophomore at Amherst. By chance, seated next to me was a famous Amherst alumnus, Dr. Calvin Plimpton, then dean of Columbia College of Physicians and Surgeons, later president of Amherst College. As the game rolled on, we introduced ourselves. During a time-out, Dr. Plimpton asked me about my career plans. I told him that I would probably be a teacher, but that from time to time I thought of being a physician. "Why don't you become a physician?" he advised. "Then you can be both."

After that remark, I hardly saw the rest of the game. Plimpton's words had provoked in me a series of endless questions: He makes sense, but could I do it? Was I smart enough? Where would I get the money for tuition? I remembered my cousin Marvin, who was a doctor. My recollection of Marvin in medical school was that he always looked tired and overworked. Was I willing to pay that price? Could I even get into medical school? Dr. Plimpton had triggered in me both passion and self-doubt.

Then I remembered Dr. Jackson Rice, the physician at my summer camp. One day, during a visit to the infirmary where I was resting with a mild flu, he surprised me by saying, "Get out of bed, get dressed, and spend the day with me. You'll get better faster."

What a prescription! I spent the day riding in the front seat of his 1946 white Buick convertible as he made house calls. Remember those? Dr. Rice asked me to remain in the car when he arrived at a patient's house—not a bad deal when you consider he brought along a stack of Superman and Batman comic books for me to read. When he returned from his visit, he told me the life story of each patient.

I still remember several of them. One involved Joe, who had suffered a stroke but was determined to walk his daughter down the aisle at her wedding in the fall. Dr. Rice said that with Joe's determination he would make his goal.

Another story involved Rosalie, who was recovering from a bleeding ulcer. Her husband was an alcoholic. Dr. Rice said that Rosalie would only get better if her husband got treatment for his alcoholism. "Seeing him destroy himself is killing her," he remarked.

Finally, there was Sally, an elderly black woman who was a home-bound invalid. Dr. Rice told me that he was looking for assistance for her daughter Betty, her caretaker. She needed to be relieved once or twice a week so that she could get out of the house. Under the stress of caring for her mother, Betty's blood pressure had risen to abnormal levels. "Unless Betty gets some help, she'll have a stroke like her mother," said Dr. Rice. We now call this "caretaker's stress" and teach about it in medical school; to Dr. Rice, it was common sense.

Too soon it was dinnertime. I ate with Dr. Rice and his family and heard more stories of patients. Each one was told with admiration and respect. After dinner, he returned me to camp. I felt perfectly well; all of my symptoms were gone. I didn't know it then, but I was "hooked" on being a physician like Jackson Rice.

On that fall afternoon when I consciously decided to be a doctor, I appreciated the gift that Dr. Rice had given me many years before. He had shown me the kind of doctor that I wanted to be. And he revealed how much a doctor needed to know about each patient's "story." He also realized that Joe's story about being present at the wedding of his daughter, Rosalie's story about her husband's alcoholism, and Betty's "truth" about what a "good" daughter should do were powerful forces in their lives. He instinctively knew that we don't just have our stories, we embody them. *We are our stories.* Jackson Rice knew this before science proved it.

Unfortunately, for a number of years, I forgot these lessons as I became a doctor.

Descartes' World

Three years after the Amherst-Williams football game, I began my medical school education, and, as such, entered a new culture. Like other cultures, as I have said, medicine contains underlying assumptions about how things are, underlying values about what is good and bad, and a system of structures and rewards that reinforces that culture.

My first year consisted of absorbing countless facts about anatomy (the structure of the body), physiology (how organ systems work), and biochemistry (how molecular systems work).

I even had classes in psychiatry. But my instructors presented mental processes that seemed to me "primitive" and completely divorced from how the rest of the body was described. We learned odd metaphoric terms like *ego, id,* and *transference.* The mind was described as an isolated entity that didn't relate to the rest of the body. I saw how liver disease could affect the kidneys; how heart disease could affect the liver. But conversations about how the mind and body interacted—what Minnie had shown me and what Jackson Rice seemed to know—were absent.

I was actually being immersed in a culture in which the mind and body were seen as separate. I didn't know it at the time, but this culture had a spiritual godfather whose name was René Descartes. This towering figure of seventeenth-century philosophy brought to medicine a mechanistic way of thinking about worldly things and events, including the function of the human body. Descartes proposed that qualities like emotion, values, goodness, courage, evil were functions of the mind, governed by separate principles from those of the machinelike body. Three hundred years later, his truths were still carried by the culture.

Until the rise of modern neuroscience in this century, this division between mind and body was the foundation of Western medical knowledge. It became the "truth" about how the world works. So as I sat in class after class in my years of medical training, I was being immersed in Descartes's world. It became the world of my certainty. Just as people before Columbus understood the world as flat, I came to understand human beings as divided entities.

The depth to which Descartes had influenced medical thinking was illustrated to me during my introductory lectures on human anatomy. Following a lecture, for example, about the anatomy of the arm, the other medical students and I would go to the dissection room to explore a motionless form. I remember feeling vaguely apprehensive about the dissection of a human being, although like my fellow students, I repressed this feeling, thinking it was not doctorly to be squeamish. As if being doctorly involved not having these feelings.

In the dissection room, I cut into the cadaver's arm with my shiny new dissection tools, comparing what I was seeing with an anatomy atlas and memorizing the arm's features—all cool, detached, and doctorly.

After the lab, I played tennis, showered, ate dinner, and spent the evening studying in textbooks what I had learned in the anatomy lab.

It wasn't until my head touched my pillow that night that the magnitude of the events of the day crystallized for me. *I had spent the day dissecting the remains of a real human being.* I remember sitting up in bed and asking myself in a frantic way, "Who was this man whose body I was dissecting?" That night I wrote the following verse, which I have kept to this day.

> Who are you, poor fellow?
> Defenseless before my probing curiosity.
>   Who are you?
> What made you laugh?
>   Who did you love?
> Did you long to look at a harvest moon?
>
> Did anyone cry for you?

I never discussed my uneasiness or showed these verses to anyone. I wanted to be a "good" doctor.

Pickles and Pulmonary Edema

Descartes' spirit became manifest again several years later when I was an intern at a university teaching hospital in Cleveland. Sam, an eighty-year-old man, had been admitted to my ward because of pulmonary edema. This is a condition where a person's heart cannot sufficiently pump the volume of blood returning to it, and consequently the lungs fill with fluid. Pulmonary edema has many causes, but the majority of cases involve either a new injury to the heart or an expansion of the blood volume, which occurs, among other reasons, because of eating too much salt.

Sam was no stranger to the medical staff. He came in almost monthly. With each admission, he would be treated and then discharged after a day or two without detection of any specific cause of the previous night's life-threatening events. This particular admission followed the same pattern. But during his first night in the ward I learned the secret behind Sam's episodes.

I found out by asking "Minnie's question." After stabilizing Sam's physiological imbalance, I asked him, "Why are you sick?" He replied, "That's your job, not mine, to find out." But I persisted and reminded him that over and over again we had tried and failed, so I repeated, "Why are you sick?" Finally, he told me. I had hit the jackpot! I had discovered the cause of Sam's attacks. It seems that Sam was unhappy with his living arrangement. Sam has lived since the death of his wife with his daughter Pat and her husband, Henry. Henry makes all the rules in the household, including what foods they eat. Sam reluctantly complies with his son-in-law's wishes. However, about once a month, when Pat and Henry go out socially, Sam hits the local deli and loads up on his favorite food—kosher pickles. Later that night his breathing becomes difficult and he ends up in the ER. That's what triggers his pulmonary edema.

I eagerly waited for rounds the next morning to present my findings to the "visit," the senior member of the ward team responsible for teaching young doctors and monitoring their performance. The visit in this case was a brilliant cardiac researcher who had done major work in electrophysiology (the study of the electrical properties of heart rhythm and beating).

As rounds began I presented the medical history and began to relate my "new" finding. Instead of praise, the visit looked at me coolly and snapped, "Sam's personal problems are something the ward social worker should be worried about, not you. It's time to move on to the next case." I thought of protesting, but I knew that my plea would fall on deaf ears. This doctor was interested in hearts and how they worked. The heart's container, the person, was not his concern. He didn't see that Sam's pulmonary edema could be treated only by a combination of dealing with his lost independence *and* with medications in an integrated way, not one or the other.

So it went throughout the rest of my internship. I would meet many doctors who were kind and empathic people. But they, like the visit, were trapped in Descartes' world. In their minds, they felt they were doing their job when they focused on the patient's physical problems to the exclusion of their concerns and emotions. That too became my orientation until over and over again, with increasing intensity, I ran into my powerlessness in the face of my patients' problems. In retrospect, I can hear the call saying, "Wake up, wake up!"

My Half-Empty Black Bag

Eventually, having completed internal medicine and specialty training (which lasted for six years after medical school) and brimful of medical knowledge about diagnosis and treatment, I was finally ready to be a doctor. I chose to practice in an innovative primary care setting, the newly opened Harvard Community Health Plan, a health maintenance organization (HMO).

Almost immediately after starting, I discovered that many of my patients' problems were not amenable to my interventions. I found myself wishing that someone would schedule a visit with me for a *real* disease, like diabetes, heart disease, or cancer. Of course some did; for them I was well prepared by my education.

But I had little to offer the many others with the nagging complaints associated with a difficult situation in life. These patients were neither sick nor crazy. For them, a mental health referral was out of the question. Patients rightfully heard such a referral as accusatory—"So, you think it's all in my head." Often the most that I could do was order diagnostic tests, make referrals, and put them on tranquilizers. During my early days of practice, Librium was the most commonly prescribed drug in the nation; later it was supplanted by Valium, then Prozac.

In fact, as I investigated the problems of patients, I found that my experience was not unique. Kurt Kronke, a researcher who was then at the Walter Reed Hospital studying patient populations, found that fourteen complaints accounted for more than half of patient visits. The complaints included fatigue and low energy, intestinal and bowel problems, difficulty with sleeping, headache, backaches, etc. Even more staggering was that physicians could find no underlying disease in almost 90 percent of people with these fourteen most common complaints.

Kronke reported that these patients had chronic life problems and this suffering was manifested in bothersome bodily symptoms and temporary emotional upset. These people went to work, cared for their families, met their obligations. They simply didn't feel well; they weren't sick in bed, but they were nonetheless suffering.

As I spoke with my colleagues about my patients and Kronke's findings, virtually all of them confessed to similar experiences in their practices. They told me they were frustrated, annoyed, or even angry with these patients! In fact, several colleagues left primary care and returned to specialty medicine where they could be "real" doctors.

Behavioral Medicine

Unlike these colleagues, my dissatisfaction fueled my desire to learn more about what was causing my patients' problems. What was going on? Why did these people have symptoms without disease? They weren't malingerers. They were really feeling pain, but why?

As I asked these questions, I began to notice mind-body connections in my own life. On those days in which I could do little to help my patients, I finished the day tired. When I was really useful, I finished with energy and vigor. My thoughts affected my body, and the state of my body altered my thinking.

My clinical instincts were soon buttressed when I began to become acquainted with a new approach in medical thinking. Beginning in the 1950s, a number of medical researchers began to formulate what they called behavioral medicine. These scientists and clinicians proposed that the mind and body were not separate, but united in an intimate way. Their research began to show that problems traditionally thought of as mental—anxiety, anger, and depression—produce bodily changes, and vice versa.

Innovators like Herbert Benson, Kenneth Pelletier, Norman Cousins, David Sobel, and Redford Williams began asking questions that had to do with the connection between mental and body states.

For example, Redford Williams, a professor at Duke Medical School, showed that "angry" people had an increased risk of heart disease when compared to "non-angry" people. Norman Cousins, the former editor of the *Saturday Review,* learned of the connection between his mood and his symptoms from his own experience with severe illness. Cousins claimed he was cured by a shift into a positive mood brought on from watching Marx Brothers' movies.

As I read these innovators' books, I was excited by the possibilities for a new approach to health and wellness. At the same time, I found it difficult to use these insights in the service of a specific patient. Knowledge of mind-body interactions set the stage, but it didn't help me in practice; I had no tools in my bag for these problems. There were few actions that a patient could take armed with my new interpretation of his or her symptoms.

Meditation, I learned, could help some people to relax; still others used it to gain awareness. But that wasn't enough. What was needed was a way to move to a new place, in effect to build a new mind and a new body that would be healthier and more at peace. I didn't have a clue as to how to do this.

So here I was, after more than a decade of training and medical practice, filled with facts and scientific techniques but unable to help a large proportion of my patients.

It was at just that point that I met Barbara at the est meeting and watched her underscore the dilemma. Obviously the mind and the body are related, but how can I work with this insight? What actions can I take or help my patients to take that will empower them in the face of their suffering?

As is so often the case in life, when I finally got to the right question, the answer appeared right in front of me. I realized it had been there all along. I simply didn't have the eyes to see it, as I'll explain in the next chapter.

My Patients

I want to introduce you now to four of my patients. (I have changed their names and identifying characteristics to protect their privacy.) In many ways, they are like thousands of people I've known over the years. As you read about these people, you'll see similarities and differences between yourself and them. Some similarities may be in the body reactions they have, some in their behaviors or personality. These people are not crazy; in fact, people like them may be your colleagues and friends—even yourself. You too have your story and it affects your life and your health.

See which patients or parts of several patients you identify with and use their learning to assist you. We will follow their stories and their reactions to the Ways to Wellness program throughout the book.

Gretchen, the Perfectionist

Gretchen is an anxious, thirty-five-year-old single woman who works as a secretary in a university department of literature. Gretchen came to my office with complaints of abdominal cramps and diarrhea. Generally, Gretchen worked despite the discomfort. But there were occasions when she missed work or social events.

Gretchen had been to several doctors and had received extensive testing, all of which had been negative. No disease could explain her symptoms. One doctor had even told Gretchen that there was "nothing wrong with her." She was inwardly furious when he said that. If she felt so bad, how could there be nothing wrong? Gretchen began to distrust doctors and her own body. She even felt a little "crazy."

Gretchen feared that the doctors were missing something. Her fear increased when she came to see me. She was now a member of an HMO, and she'd heard these organizations have a reputation for withholding necessary tests and referrals.

As I talked with Gretchen, she revealed that she had graduated from her state university, where she had done well, but "not as well as I could if I were healthy." She had taken a secretarial position until "I could get myself straightened out." I asked her what she meant by that and she said, "You know what I mean, feeling well." Ten years later, Gretchen was still a secretary.

Throughout her childhood, Gretchen's parents had stressed "better, better, best" at all times. Her mother was a perfectionist, and so was Gretchen. She was trained in strict fundamentalist religious views. Not only did her parents expect her to perform perfectly, but, in keeping with their midwestern traditions, they taught her to be calm, orderly, and unemotional. To them, any outward display of emotion was a sign of weakness.

Nonetheless, whenever Gretchen had multiple tasks to do, or when she was doing something for the first time, she would become highly nervous and agitated and tense in her belly. Gretchen would snap at others, then feel guilty for her behavior. Making errors in her professional life was anathema to her. So she often worked late at night, going over and over her work. Her boss praised Gretchen for her accuracy.

In her personal life Gretchen's perfectionism generated constant worry: What to wear? What to cook? What to do? Will people like me? Will they approve of me? Learning was difficult for Gretchen; it's hard to be perfect when you're a beginner, so she avoided career advancement and continued as a secretary.

Her social life was very limited. She rarely dated. When she became emotionally or even physically aroused, her Calvinistic history loudly screamed through her body—Stop!

Walter, the Angry Man

Walter is a forty-eight-year-old taxi driver. He had had two heart attacks when his cardiologist referred him to me.

Walter grew up in a Catholic family with a father, mother, two brothers, and two sisters. His father expected each child to "pull his or her own weight." Walter began to earn money at an early age. His father laid down strict rules regarding the children's conduct. Breaking them meant facing their father's rage, which, when he was drinking, was terrifying and involved physical and emotional abuse.

By the time Walter was eighteen, his father was drinking heavily. Walter joined the army to escape his home life. He became a master sergeant and served in Vietnam, where he was wounded during the Tet offensive. Over time, Walter became disillusioned with the war as he witnessed countless atrocities.

After the war ended, Walter came home. Twice married, he drifted from job to job until settling on taxi driving. He drank heavily on occasion, but not steadily. He was constantly angry and bitter about life. "You can't trust anyone" was his motto.

When he was in his early forties, Walter had his two heart attacks; during the second one he almost died and required coronary surgery. Even after the surgery, his moments of anger and rage were often accompanied by chest pain. Walter's physician referred him to the Ways to Wellness course to help him manage stress better.

At the first class meeting, Walter became angry at something another patient said. His face grew red, his voice loud, and his manner harsh. When I asked him if he had this feeling often, Walter angrily answered, "What feeling?" I pointed to his body tension. He replied, "Of course I do. The world is filled with jerks!"

Walter rattled on about his grievances against his wife, his doctor, drivers on the road, the dispatcher at work, and his taxi passengers. As he recounted this tale of woe, I again asked him how often he felt this way—tense, taut, wanting to strike out. "Dozens of times a day!" he said angrily.

Robert, the High Achiever

Robert is a twenty-eight-year-old lawyer who came to see me at the urging of a relative who was also my patient.

Robert told me he suffered from stomach pain and insomnia. The stomach pain had been getting worse for weeks and was now constant. His insomnia was so bad that he slept only one or two hours a night. He got out of bed exhausted every morning. Robert's fatigue and pain were now interfering with his professional and personal life. Expecting his first child, Robert feared that there would be "just more work to do."

Robert is the oldest son of a Jewish family. Academic excellence was expected of him. He had fulfilled these expectations—he graduated at the top of his class from an Ivy League college and was on the law review at an Ivy League law school. Despite academic achievement, learning did not come easily to Robert. He paid a price—long hours of work, little social life, and a continuously nagging sense of anxiety and dread.

When he finally joined a major Boston law firm, Robert hoped that the pressure would ease up. Instead, sensing his ambition, the firm's senior partners gave him some of their most difficult cases.

This pressed Robert to the limit. He lay in bed at night thinking of alternate ways to handle each problem. He was plagued by "what ifs." For Robert, the level of uncertainty was intolerable. He was fearful of talking to senior partners about the cases because he thought this would make him look dumb. So he never used the expertise of others. He worked alone. Robert's fear of failure provoked a continual state of anxiety. He was in a bind between the high expectations he had for himself and his abilities. He saw no way out except more hard work. But there was never enough time.

Robert found himself "jammed," feeling ill, and for the first time feared he would be unsuccessful. He feared he couldn't meet either his or his firm's expectations.

Linda, the Depressed Woman

Linda is a fifty-five-year-old mother of four and the grandmother of three. She came to my office complaining of fatigue, low energy, and little interest in life. The things that used to give her pleasure were now boring.

Linda grew up in a large family that was rigid and disciplined. When she made mistakes she was called "stupid" and sometimes embarrassed in public. Her mother let her know clearly that she was not her favorite. Linda never remembers being praised or encouraged to try something new and challenging.

She made it through junior college. Because Linda loved children, she wanted to finish her education so she could be an elementary school teacher. But she never got around to it after she married. Aimlessly drifting from one "duty" to the next was her modus operandi. Linda was, in a sense, a slave to her environment. She lived as if she didn't have the right to freedom or dignity.

Linda's husband, Jack, was a traveling salesman. He was away much of the time, and when he returned from his business trips he was usually tired, irritable, and demanding. He often criticized Linda for the way she kept the house. When Jack did this, he reminded Linda of her mother and she felt terrible. Linda saw the future as hopeless. "Is this all there is?" she asked.

Pretest
"You Are What You Say"

Before we proceed to the first exercise section, I invite you to take this brief test. It is designed to help you begin to think about your strengths and learning points, and to assist you in developing awareness of how your thoughts and feelings affect your health.

First, you assess yourself with the test. Then you can compare yourself to the four patients that I have introduced to you. Remember, what we are doing here is building a base of awareness as the first step in your learning. Observe any reactions you might have to this test. You may feel resistant, guilty, angry, or some other emotion. Just observe your automatic response without judgment.

Be as honest as you can. At the end of the book, after you have read, learned, and practiced, I provide an opportunity for you to test yourself again to note progress and to guide your further learning.

How to Use the Test

These tests allow you to assess yourself in three important and basic dimensions of human life—and therefore health: **self-efficacy** (a "can-do" attitude that some people may have), **social ease** (the comfort and intimacy that some people have with others), and **emotional skills** (the ability that some people have to know their emotions and use their emotional reactions constructively in relationships).

Assessing yourself in these three areas will:

□ help you focus your learning
□ introduce you to the notion of the mind-body connection
□ allow you to note your own progress in learning.

Here is how the test works. Each of the three dimensions has two components. For example, self-efficacy is comprised of ambition and also of the ability to learn and change. Can you see that "can-do" people tend to be ambitious and can also learn and change? They are flexible and take hold of new projects in life with confidence.

So, to assess yourself in self-efficacy, you first turn to each of the separate scales, Ambition and Learning, and rate yourself on each. Be honest, not self-critical or arrogant. Rate yourself from o to 8 on each scale.

Then go to the Self-efficacy graph and find the horizontal bar labeled Ambition. Notice how at the bottom it is divided into boxes numbered 0 to 8. Place a mark on this horizontal scale that corresponds to how you rated yourself on the Ambition scale.

Now return to the Self-efficacy graph and find the vertical bar labeled Learning. The scale for learning is on both the right and left sides of the graph. Find the number that corresponds to how you rated yourself in learning and make a mark on the vertical scale.

Now, to determine your self-efficacy score, draw a vertical line from your number on the Ambition scale and a horizontal line from your number on the Learning scale. Draw an "X" in the box where the two lines intersect.

For example, the person who took this sample test rated herself a "7" in Ambition and a "3" in Learning. So, she marked a 7 on the horizontal scale and 3 on the vertical one. Her two numbers intersected in quadrant 2, where the "X" is shown. Now she could see how she was doing in this important self-efficacy, or "can-do," characteristic. I have provided "typical profiles" of people whose results fall in each of the quadrants. For example, people whose results fall in quadrant 2 are often frustrated. They have lofty visions, but do not attain them because they are poor learners. This could be useful and might lead to the question, "How can I improve my ability to learn?"

Now you are ready to take this pretest.

After you take the test, you will have available several useful pieces of information:

☐ What quadrant you fall into (see descriptions).
☐ How far from center or extreme you are in that quadrant. The farther you are from center, the more dominant that quality is in your life. This is neither good nor bad. It's just the way it is.
☐ How you compare with the four patients in the book. Their tests appear after the blank tests you'll be filling out. You will be able to see which one(s) you resemble most closely and follow their learning as a model and inspiration for your own.

I also describe the behavior characteristic of each of the four quadrants and give a general description of the trait in question.

Use this material as a guide, consciousness raiser, and inspiration— *not* as an invalidation.

Example of filled in
Self-efficacy (a "Can-Do" Attitude)

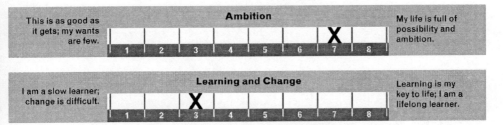

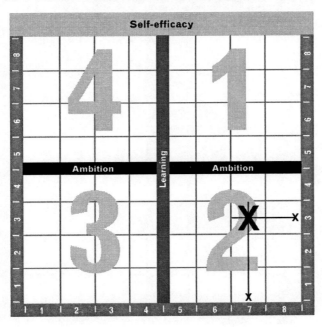

I. Self-efficacy.

This behavioral characterization reflects two dimensions of human existence: the presence of ambition, and the sense that one can make the changes necessary to achieve that ambition. Together they allow a person to pursue meaningful goals. Self-efficacy and meaning are major health enhancers; their absence is a health risk.

Self-efficacy (a "Can-Do" Attitude)

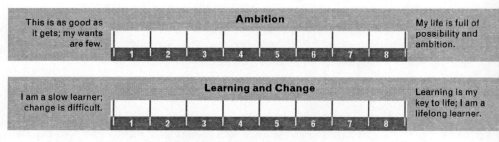

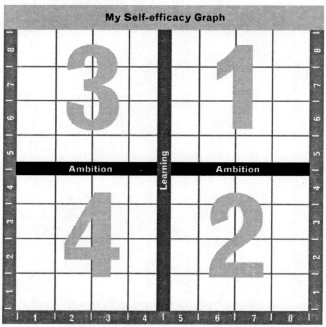

Typical Profile of Each Quadrant

1. **Learner:** You make personal declarations and back them up with learning and change. You achieve success and may lead others.
2. **Frustrated:** You have lofty visions but can't mobilize to fulfill them. Frustration is common.
3. **Pedant:** Learners without ambition "stockpile" information and are often boring and pedantic.
4. **Resigned:** You are without ambition and change is difficult. Life looks bleak and repetitive.

Social Ease
(Comfort and Intimacy with Others)

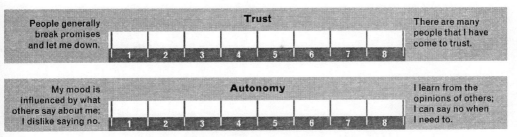

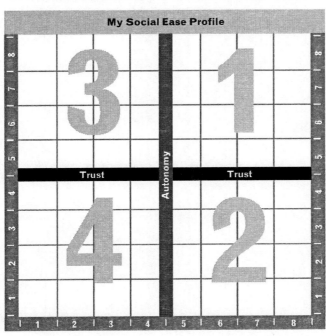

II. Social Ease.

I have combined two dimensions in this way of looking at human behavior. The first is trust: Are you able to enter into trusting relationships, even intimate ones? Second, are you able to retain autonomy and dignity in linguistic interactions with others: to decline gracefully, to listen to the assessments of others constructively, and to make requests when necessary? These two dimensions taken together define what I call social ease, and represent a major health enhancer or risk factor.

Emotional Skills
(Dealing with Feelings)

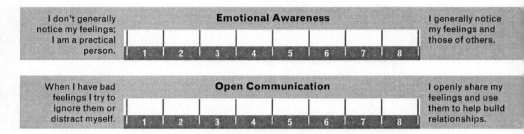

Emotional Awareness

I don't generally notice my feelings; I am a practical person.

I generally notice my feelings and those of others.

| 1 | 2 | 3 | 4 | 5 | 6 | 7 | 8 |

Open Communication

When I have bad feelings I try to ignore them or distract myself.

I openly share my feelings and use them to help build relationships.

| 1 | 2 | 3 | 4 | 5 | 6 | 7 | 8 |

Your Emotional Skills Profile

Open and Responsible

Open and Responsible

Emotional Awareness

Typical Profile of Each Quadrant

1. **Effective partner:** You trust and enter relationships and intimacy, but keep your sense of self intact.
2. **Dependent:** You cling to others for meaning and direction.
3. **Lone Ranger:** You are independent and unattached, the American ideal.
4. **Isolated:** You distrust others and avoid intimacy. Eventually you isolate yourself.

III. Emotional Skills.

This set of behavioral skills has recently been described by Daniel Goleman, the author of the best-seller *Emotional Intelligence*. Emotional intelligence (EI) appears to be important for success and health.

In general, there are two aspects of emotional intelligence. First, people with high EI are aware of their feelings moment by moment. They honor, respect, and are aware of their own emotional life and that of others. Second, they take care of their emotional lives. When they are in discomfort they make that known to others in a nonblaming but behavior-changing way. Additionally, they attend to the discomfort of others.

Typical Profile in Each Quadrant

1. **Emotional intelligence:** Good partners, team players, leaders.
2. **Emotional "bull in china shop":** Open, but very little awareness of emotional life of self or others. Unaware of reaction of others to his/her expressiveness.
3. **Silent sufferer:** Feels social pain, but "stuck" with it.
4. **Alexithymia:** Unaware of own feelings, closed to feelings of others. People in this category are disconnected from intimate relationships and often are mechanical in their behavior.

The four patients described in chapter 1 took this test. Here are their results. Notice which ones are different from or similar to your own, and follow their learning in the course of the book as an aid to your endeavors.

Gretchen

Gretchen is a perfectionist, so lofty goals are a threat to her and a setup for not being "good enough." Learning produces great anxiety—she might make mistakes. She trusts people but defers to their judgment so that she is continually placing herself in an anxiously dependent role. She walls herself off from her feelings and is closed about them to herself and others.

Self-efficacy (a "Can-Do" Attitude)

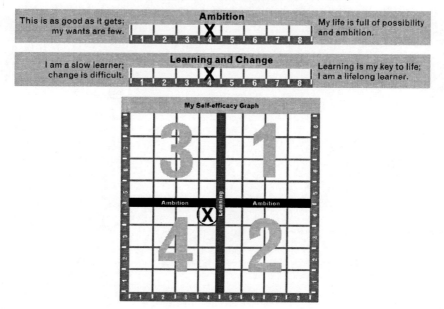

Social Ease (Comfort and Intimacy with Others)

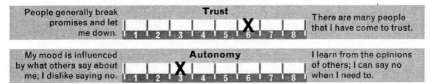

People generally break promises and let me down.	**Trust**	There are many people that I have come to trust.
My mood is influenced by what others say about me; I dislike saying no.	**Autonomy**	I learn from the opinions of others; I can say no when I need to.

My Social Ease Profile

Emotional Skills (Dealing with Feelings)

I don't generally notice my feelings; I am a practical person.	**Emotional Awareness**	I generally notice my feelings and those of others.
When I have bad feelings I try to ignore them or distract myself.	**Open Communication**	I openly share my feelings and use them to help build relationships.

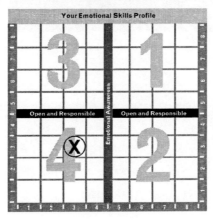

Your Emotional Skills Profile

Robert

Robert scores a lukewarm 1 on self-efficacy. His goals are somewhat ambitious, but are given "to" him by others; they are not his own. He looks to others for approval and judgment, therefore is dependent and continually vulnerable. He is aware of his feelings, in fact suffers with them, but can do little to change matters in his life.

Self-efficacy (a "Can-Do" Attitude)

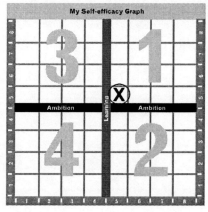

Social Ease (Comfort and Intimacy with Others)

People generally break promises and let me down.

Trust

1 2 3 4 X 5 6 7 8

There are many people that I have come to trust.

My mood is influenced by what others say about me; I dislike saying no.

Autonomy

1 X 2 3 4 5 6 7 8

I learn from the opinions of others; I can say no when I need to.

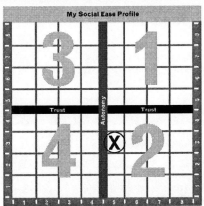

My Social Ease Profile

Emotional Skills (Dealing with Feelings)

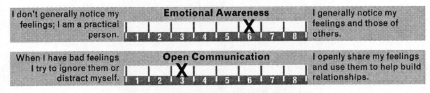

I don't generally notice my feelings; I am a practical person.

Emotional Awareness

1 2 3 4 5 X 6 7 8

I generally notice my feelings and those of others.

When I have bad feelings I try to ignore them or distract myself.

Open Communication

1 X 2 3 4 5 6 7 8

I openly share my feelings and use them to help build relationships.

Your Emotional Skills Profile

Walter

Walter does have ambitions and is a fairly good learner. However, he is profoundly distrustful of people. He angers easily, has little insight into how this affects others, and cannot express his anger constructively, so he "strikes out" at others.

Self-efficacy (a "Can-Do" Attitude)

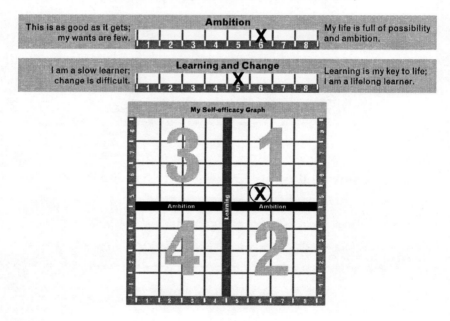

Social Ease (Comfort and Intimacy with Others)

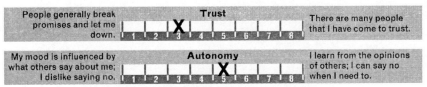

People generally break promises and let me down.

Trust

|X| 1 | 2 | 3 | 4 | 5 | 6 | 7 | 8 |

There are many people that I have come to trust.

My mood is influenced by what others say about me; I dislike saying no.

Autonomy

| 1 | 2 | 3 | 4 |X| 5 | 6 | 7 | 8 |

I learn from the opinions of others; I can say no when I need to.

My Social Ease Profile

Emotional Skills (Dealing with Feelings)

I don't generally notice my feelings; I am a practical person.

Emotional Awareness

| 1 | 2 |X| 3 | 4 | 5 | 6 | 7 | 8 |

I generally notice my feelings and those of others.

When I have bad feelings I try to ignore them or distract myself.

Open Communication

| 1 | 2 | 3 | 4 | 5 | 6 |X| 7 | 8 |

I openly share my feelings and use them to help build relationships.

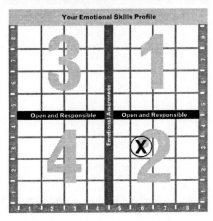

Your Emotional Skills Profile

Linda

Linda is deeply resigned. She has little sense of meaning, passion, or self-confidence. She is aware of her miserable feelings, but cannot act on them in a positive way. She trusts people in a way, but is shattered by their opinions, judgments, and requests.

Self-efficacy (a "Can-Do" Attitude)

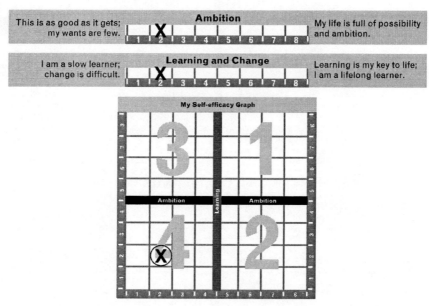

Social Ease (Comfort and Intimacy with Others)

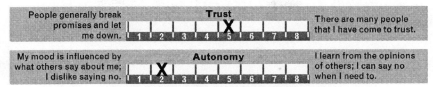

People generally break promises and let me down. | **Trust** | There are many people that I have come to trust.

My mood is influenced by what others say about me; I dislike saying no. | **Autonomy** | I learn from the opinions of others; I can say no when I need to.

My Social Ease Profile

Emotional Skills (Dealing with Feelings)

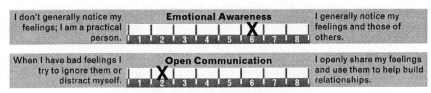

I don't generally notice my feelings; I am a practical person. | **Emotional Awareness** | I generally notice my feelings and those of others.

When I have bad feelings I try to ignore them or distract myself. | **Open Communication** | I openly share my feelings and use them to help build relationships.

Your Emotional Skills Profile

EXERCISES

Major Points in Chapter 1

□ You see and act in a world that reveals itself to you as a reflection of your background beliefs and assumptions. The world mirrors your mind. You see what you *can* see.

□ My grandmother Minnie was "uneducated" by American standards—she was brought up in an Eastern European peasant environment, not the world of advanced Western science and medicine. Because of this she "saw" differently. She looked at "illness" from a very different perspective than that of a physician. Minnie carried an old wisdom that contained spiritual and practical explanations for why people became ill.

This led my grandmother to ask the provocative and unconventional question "Why are you sick?" when I returned from school with the "flu." For her, the question made all the sense in the world. People get sick when they're upset.

This experience and her question stuck with me throughout my medical training. It seemed true, even though it didn't fit the scientific viewpoint in which I was immersed.

□ In medical school I learned the Cartesian model of scientific thinking, which separates the mind from the body. From this perspective, medicine's "common sense," doctors have made enormous discoveries and uncovered fundamental and useful insights. It helped doctors become vastly better diagnosticians of physical illness.

□ When I began medical practice I quickly discovered that my patients' suffering could not be understood only from a strictly disease orientation. Many were symptomatic, but not ill.

□ As part of my search for answers on how to be a better doctor, I attended a seminar at the recommendation of a friend. There I watched a fellow participant named Barbara experience an asthma attack. To my amazement, a conversation between Barbara and the seminar's leader arrested her attack. This experience profoundly altered my notion of healing. I couldn't explain what had happened. However, the incident motivated me to seek an explanation that I could use for others and for myself.

□ I introduced four patients—Gretchen, a perfectionist; Walter, an angry man; Robert, a high achiever; and Linda, a depressed woman—

to illustrate health problems outside the scope of my "black bag." I'll return repeatedly to these patients throughout the book to illustrate their learning and their progress. You can learn from their journey, including seeing what they learned in the workbook chapters.

□ As the chapter ends, I embark on a new path of learning, and share this with you.

The Awareness Exercise

The practice of meditation is a major element in the development of *awareness*. All of the world's great religions have a "meditative" aspect. In Buddhism, meditation is the central element. In other religions, prayer and ritual offer moments of meditation and reflection.

Meditation has two major benefits. First, it helps you to achieve a relaxed and open body. A body in this state facilitates learning, listening, and being present.

Second, and most important, meditation supports and fosters self-reflection. It helps you to witness and observe the way your automatic thinking shapes your behavior and your world. The more you meditate, the more "space" is created for observing and letting go of past ways of acting, and for learning new ways of being.

As you use the workbook exercises in each chapter over the next weeks, I urge you to develop the practice of meditation. Its benefits deepen with repetition. Each time you do it, the experience will be different because you're different in every moment—one moment tired, one moment joyful, one moment harassed by all you have to do. You'll begin to observe your repertoire of learned reactions in life.

When you begin to meditate, do it for five or ten minutes. If you can, increase this duration to twenty minutes. Look at this time as a gift to yourself. Do your meditation the same time each day and, if possible, follow it with your exercises for reflection, which I'll explain later in this chapter.

I began meditation at a Tibetan Buddhist center when I was forty-five years old. After the first session, I went home and started meditating enthusiastically. After a week, I didn't want to do it anymore. I asked myself why I had gone to the center in the first place. I remember resisting this intrusion into my day. It was already full; how could I find twenty minutes to spare?

But I decided to continue meditating because I was committed to learning a new approach to healing. I became more and more regular in the practice. Gradually, meditation became of greater and greater value to me. In fact, it now enables me to function much more efficiently and peacefully throughout my day. See if this doesn't happen to you.

How to Meditate

Here is one way to meditate.

Sit comfortably in a firm chair with a straight back, or on a cushion on the floor with your legs crossed. Sit alertly, not stiffly. Find a place where your body feels centered, not leaning in any direction. Hold your head in an alert position, not slumped forward. Let your jaw relax; it may drop and your lips may part. Just center yourself for a few moments.

Now let your eyes fall shut, or you can simply let your gaze soften. Maintain your posture and stay centered.

Next, begin deep breathing in the following way. With each in breath, let your belly expand (you may have to loosen your belt or clothing), and with each out breath, let your belly fall. Breathe in and out, regularly and deeply.

Do this for a few moments, then check your posture. If you find you've slumped, recenter yourself. Look for any tension in your body and see if you're willing to just relax. Keep breathing deeply and easily.

Now, gently bring your attention to your breath. Watch it, witness it with a nonjudging mind. Let your awareness "ride" your breath as a rider rides a horse. In and out.

From time to time you may experience a sound or sensation of something outside of you. Notice what it is with a nonjudging mind and return your awareness to your breathing.

Your may feel a body sensation. Be aware of it fully and then return to your breathing.

You may notice your mood or emotion; just be aware of it without analysis or judgment.

Thoughts will arise. Notice them and return to your breathing.

Keep doing this, breathing and noticing, each time returning to your breathing until your twenty minutes are up.

See, it's really easy, and very natural.

As you begin to do this exercise, reread the instructions for each of the first few times, then do the exercise.

When I began meditating I continually asked myself, "Am I doing this right?" When you begin, you may find that question popping into your mind. If this happens, continue to follow the directions and focus on the statement "Notice the thought and return to your breathing." You may be beginning to see that you are a "doing it right" machine like I was.

Often I have these thoughts when I meditate: "I don't have time for this" or "When will this be over?" Again, if those thoughts occur to you, follow the directions, complete the twenty minutes, and ask yourself, "Do I live my life as if time is scarce?" or "Is taking care of myself the last item on my list of priorities?"

Use this exercise to create a mirror for self-reflection.

Automatic Writing

Automatic writing is a powerful tool for reflection and learning. It's a way of circumventing the editing mind, the part of you that says, "I'm too smart to do that" or "I shouldn't say that." It's a form of meditation in writing.

Normally when you write, you have something to say to an imagined or real reader. In automatic writing, you pick a topic and write at a fast pace for a timed period, say five minutes. Whatever happens, you keep writing until your time is up, even if nonsense comes out.

Automatic writing is a practice that pays great dividends. When you write your thoughts down, they become clearer to you. Such clarity is vital in discovering your "truth." Automatic writing has another benefit. If you write as rapidly as you can, without stopping to think and ponder, you'll see amazing associations between your memories, thoughts, feelings, perceptions, and actions. Your pen may go to strange places, but there are no accidents. The places you go reflect your system of thought. Respect what you write. This exercise is a wonderful way to expand awareness of your "system of thought."

I first experienced the power of automatic writing when I took a course in self-awareness at the Cambridge Center for Adult Education. The course focused on exploring themes in an adult's life. As I did it, I was amazed at what came out of my pen, things that I had long forgotten.

I wrote about an asthma attack I had when I was two years old. I remembered feeling tremendously alone, and very frightened. Later, when I asked my mother about this incident, she confirmed that it did happen.

My mother explained that when she and my father ran their family business, they often had to leave our house at the same time. They would wait until I fell asleep before leaving me with a sitter. During one of their absences I had my first asthma attack. My mother now thinks that my fear at being left led to the attack. I remembered this during automatic writing. This memory helped me to understand the connection between fear and illness in my own life.

How to Practice Automatic Writing

1. Write in the space provided in this book or, if you prefer, get a journal or notebook.
2. Find a quiet place for writing.
3. Choose a topic—a particular incident from your childhood, hopes for a new career, what you saw on the bus. You can write about something you consciously want to explore, or let a topic "come" to you. Or pick a theme or reaction that keeps coming up in the exercises. Next, focus on your topic, not just your thoughts but also the feelings in your body, your sensations, your emotions around this topic, etc.
4. Write for at least five minutes, longer if you wish.
5. Write down whatever comes up; don't edit.
6. Keep writing until the time is up. You may want to set a timer, clock, or watch near you to time the exercise.
7. Don't let your pen or pencil stop writing. Keep going rapidly. Don't think, then write; just write, write, write.

When you're done, take a moment to read and reflect on what you wrote. Did you see anything new? About yourself? About your body and your history? Just notice what came up for you when you set your pen free.

Automatic Writing

Exercises for Reflection and Learning

You as a Learner—Exercise One

In this exercise, I want you to reflect on your experiences with learning, especially moments when you had to stretch yourself to learn, i.e., a challenging learning experience, or one that placed pressure on you. I want you to encounter the reactions that you may have about learning and how, as you continue, you gain confidence in your ability to learn.

Close your eyes and imagine an event at home, at work, in school, or in your private life when you were challenged by a learning task. It may have been in chemistry, physics, a foreign language, or a complex new procedure such as when you learned to drive with your father or an instructor. Close your eyes and imagine this experience.

Reflect on what your thoughts were when challenged by the task. What did you say to yourself?

□ *When I did this exercise for the first time, I remembered learning to use a computer. I was the only person in the class who had no computer experience. I was embarrassed and self-conscious. I found it very difficult to pay attention because I was so distracted by my own thoughts of embarrassment. This exercise helped me see that I'm embarrassed when I don't know something. I don't like to be a beginner in public.*

Notice what your body feels like when you remember a learning moment when you were challenged. Was there any tension or fear in your body?
What consequences did you anticipate? Success or failure?
How has your attitude toward learning shaped your life?
Take notes here to use when you do automatic writing later on.

Notes
(You as a Learner—Exercise One)

You as a Learner—Exercise Two

In this exercise I want you to learn something new and observe yourself while learning it.

Pick a learning task for yourself that is a stretch for you but that you would genuinely like to accomplish. And make sure you can learn it in a relatively short period. It may be to bake bread or balance a checkbook, assemble an outdoor swing set, learn how to juggle, or master a new computer program. It may be learning to use a new camera, fill out a tax form, or memorize a new poem. Make it the kind of activity you might avoid with statements to yourself like "Bread baking is for women" or "I'll let my husband balance the checkbook" or "I'll call the store and have them assemble the swing." Or "There are plenty of people around the office who know this software program." Or "I'm too old to start a new hobby."

As you engage with the learning, listen to your thoughts, your background conversation. Notice the voices in your head that are like a sports announcer commenting on your performance from the broadcasting booth. Notice any urge to give up, or an attitude that says, "I need to get this right quickly" or "This is too hard!"

As you enter learning, become aware of any changes in your body, such as muscle tension, sweating, a pounding heart, fatigue, sleepiness, boredom, panic, etc. Also, check on your mood. Is it joyful, embarrassed, frustrated, engaged?

When you finish the exercise, ask yourself what you learned about how you learn. Then ask, "How has this automatic reaction affected my life?"

□ *I personally tried juggling. I bought a set of juggling balls and began. (You can do this with tennis balls, or golf balls.) I noticed that my body reacts in a stereotyped way when I perceive the challenge of learning. I was alone, so I wasn't embarrassed. But I experienced a tense, jaw-forward, anxious kind of propelling into the work. I had a strong sense of urgency to "get it" quickly. And I noticed that my body became tense, which made the juggling, or "getting it," even more difficult. Each time I dropped a ball, I automatically said, "Damn it," as if I should know how to juggle genetically.*

□ *These same attitudes have come up all of my life when I begin to learn. For years they consumed tremendous energy, because I suppressed these feelings and forced myself to learn anyway. In medical school, I expended more than the average amount of effort in learning. Then I began to become aware of these reactions, to observe them, and accept that this reaction to learning was a product of my history—it's the past that I bring to the present. I became more aware of the reaction and accepted it. As I did, its grip on me loosened.*

Your reactions may have either propelled your learning forward or impeded it. See if you can discern certain patterns in yourself as a learner.

Take notes on what you saw here. Use them later in your automatic writing.

Notes
(You as a Learner—Exercise Two)

You as a Learner—Exercise Three

Close your eyes and recall a time when you were learning from a teacher. It may have been a skating teacher, a dance instructor, a math or language teacher, a mentor at work, or a driving instructor. It may have been at home, at school, at your workplace—any moment of learning will do for this exercise.

Now imagine that the teacher is criticizing what you're doing—you've made some mistakes. Notice your reactions. Are you defensive? Are you embarrassed? Are you grateful?

Even though we need and want teachers, our bodies sometimes react negatively to the correction of a teacher. Why do you suppose this is so? What kind of person would react defensively to a teacher, especially when he or she wants to learn?

□ *For me, the approval of teachers was always a central concern. I needed to do it right the first time. I saw their comments as a statement that I should have done better. Negative assessments upset me deeply. I took their judgments not as learning aids, but as judgments of my innate ability.*

I still remember my first grade teacher, Ms. Greene, who was a stern-faced perfectionist. She was continually on my back to do things right. I was energetic and reasonably intelligent. But Ms. Greene "taught" me that learning was like walking on eggs. Even as I write about this today, my stomach tightens up. My body remembers.

What was your characteristic relationship to your teachers? To different kinds of teachers?

Notes
(You as a Learner—Exercise Three)

You as a Learner—Exercise Four

Here are some more questions about yourself as a learner. If you're tired now, come back to them later when you're fresh, because they'll show you a lot. First, read them quickly just to get a sense of their content. Then read each one slowly, pausing for reflection. Turn your awareness on yourself and notice what is triggered for you, in your body, your thoughts, your emotions.

Then read them a third time and try to answer this question: "When did I become that way?"

Remember that the context of your learning is awareness and acceptance. Your goal is to look fully at yourself without judgment. No blame, okay?

1. Are you willing to admit that you don't know something, or is this difficult for you?
2. Is it difficult for you to admit that someone else knows something that you don't know?
3. Do you have problems with having someone teach you, including criticizing your performance? What are your reactions?
4. Do you think that you can learn anything that you set your mind to and have a good teacher for? Or is your learning limited?
5. What mood do you fall into when you begin to learn something difficult?

6. Are you embarrassed about making mistakes?

7. How are you about practicing, the discipline necessary to learn?

We each have a great biological capacity for learning. The internal conversations that you've been examining in this section are about you as a learner, your strengths and barriers. You have to be aware of them and paradoxically embrace and accept them if you're going to change.

Take notes on what you've seen about yourself.

Notes
(You as a Learner—Exercise Four)

Automatic Writing, Revisited

First, review the notes that you made about yourself in the preceeding learning exercises. Read your notes slowly and thoughtfully.

Then, write nonstop for five minutes in the following pages, or on a blank sheet in your journal, about what you see about yourself as a learner. How has learning been for you? What is your history as a learner? How have your attitudes affected your learning history? Where did these attitudes come from? What are your physical reactions to learning?

Remember, make these judgments without blame or resentment.

Automatic Writing

Now go back and read what you wrote. What did you see?

As you continue with these workbook chapters, return from time to time to these exercises and to your notes and automatic writings about yourself as a learner. It's important that you do so. We're working to build an awareness and acceptance of yourself as a learner, however your history has shaped you. The purpose of these and all subsequent exercises is to put you into a position where you can learn more effectively.

The Experiences of My Patients in Doing These Exercises

Gretchen, the Perfectionist

Gretchen recalled learning to drive. Her father was her instructor. She remembered their initial lesson together took place in front of their house. She was seated in the driver's seat for the first time, excited at the prospect of driving, but fearful that she wouldn't know how.

As they drove, her father instructed, "Let up the clutch pedal slowly." Gretchen asked, "How slowly?" He replied, "You'll see." As she tried to follow his instructions, the car lurched and bucked forward. Her father yelled, "Too fast!" Gretchen now became frightened. On her second try, the car bucked again. Her father screamed, "You stupid girl! You should be able to do this! You'll ruin the car."

By now, Gretchen was terrified and ashamed of herself. Her stomach cramped up. She put on the brake and jumped out of the car. She raced back toward their house, shouting behind her, "I have to go to the bathroom." She was frightened, ashamed, and miserable.

Gretchen refused to do the second "You as a Learner" exercise. She said, "Why should I put myself through that stress?"

She later observed that novelty and learning always provoked this reaction in her. Ironically, Gretchen avoided learning situations and in this sense made herself "stupid." Can you see how she'd created a self-fulfilling prophecy? What is yours?

Walter, the Angry Man

Walter had trouble with these exercises. He said, "Why should I do these things? I don't know if you know what you're doing."

I asked him if distrust showed up for him in other contexts. He said, "Sure! Most people can't be trusted." As he said this, his face and neck flushed and his voice grew louder. He was becoming angry.

"Is anger a good mood for learning?" I asked him.

He was confused by my question and suspiciously blurted out, "What the hell are you talking about?"

I repeated the question in a different form. "If you remain angry and distrustful, what do you think your chances of learning anything in this course are?"

He paused for a minute and said, "Not great, I guess." I agreed and invited him to observe his reactions to learning. He wasn't happy with my request, but sat down quietly.

This reaction was perfect for Walter's learning. By observing his reactions to the learning situation of the class, he was doing the exercise. The angry, distrustful learner that he was began to surface as a barrier to his own learning. In the mirror of awareness, he was able to observe himself as a learner.

How are you similar to or different from Walter as a learner?

Robert, the High Achiever

Robert started the homework energetically, but soon became concerned about whether he was getting it right. "Am I meditating correctly?" he nervously asked me.

I told him to follow the instructions and notice what happened. He repeated, "But am I doing it right?"

I said, "Wonderful! Just notice that."

Robert became irritated with me. "Why won't you tell me what to do?"

I replied, "I'm more interested in your question."

I reminded Robert that what we were doing in class was becoming familiar with ourselves as learners. With awareness and acceptance, we could free ourselves to learn.

"Are you a 'doing it right' machine?" I asked Robert.

"Yes, all my life," he answered honestly.

I pointed out to him that learning always involves making mistakes. His lifelong "doing it right" attitude constricted his choices; he could either avoid learning or feel threatened by learning.

Robert said, "That's me. Learning makes me crazy. It's a constant battle with myself."

Linda, the Depressed Woman

Linda didn't do the homework. She said, "What good will it do me?"

I said that I couldn't answer that question, but that the program had helped others. It certainly wouldn't help her if she didn't do the exercises.

"Nothing ever works for me," she replied.

I answered that I didn't believe that for two reasons. First, she hadn't experienced everything in life, so the statement itself was ungrounded. It expressed her mood of pessimism rather than reality. And second, as a physician and knowing what I know about biology, I believed that every living person can learn.

I challenged her with the following question: "If you're so certain that you can't learn, and that nothing works, why did you enroll in this class? Somewhere deep inside, you know that life could be better."

Linda looked at me intensely for the first time, right into my eyes. "You know what I mean?" I asked.

"I think so," was her response as she slumped into her chair.

I urged her to try to stay in touch with that spark of hope and power that led her to the class and take that with her into the homework.

She said she would try.

As you do the exercises and place yourself in the role of learner, begin to observe yourself gently. New observations may raise regrets or guilt. Try not to go there. Simply witness and take these learnings forward into the next chapters.

We Are Animals, but
We Have Forgotten

We think with the whole body.
—TAISEN DESHIMARU, Zen roshi

That's what I want to call thought, which includes emotion,
body state, physical reaction, perception and everything else.
—DAVID BOHM, physicist

Barbara's response during the est seminar showed me something I had never before been aware of—the *patterned reactivity* of the human body. When Barbara "saw" a person who looked like an
authority figure with control over her—Irving the course leader—she
had a tremendous emotional reaction and an asthma attack. She had
probably behaved this way thousands of times before, always in the same
manner, without any awareness of her role in creating or generating her
reaction. Barbara believed the Irvings in her life were causing her to respond this way. She was a victim.

In fact, Barbara responded without ever thinking about her role in
her reaction. If I had questioned Barbara about what happened, she
would have probably said that Irving "was cruel, controlling, and mean
and caused my attack." Barbara *did not* have the following conversation
with herself before having her attack: "This man acts in a way that implies that he controls me by telling me what to do. This reminds me of
my father, who always told me what to do. I'm filled with fear and anger;
anger worked when I was young to keep my father off balance and to
stop him from telling me what to do. If my anger now doesn't stop Irving from trying to control me, maybe an asthma attack will. Then Irving

will leave me alone." Barbara absolutely never had this conversation consciously, I'll bet on it. But the reaction issued forth from her body as automatically as music from a jukebox: when you press the same number, you always get the same song.

Barbara is not alone in her unthinking reaction to events in her life. We all are Barbaras in our own special way. Let me tell you something I recently noticed about myself. A major theme of my life has been about personal achievement, getting ahead, and being right. I have embodied this theme since my earliest days. I was the firstborn son of a first-generation American family who struggled to survive the Great Depression. I share this orientation with many others of my generation, but exhibit it in my own personal way. The dream of my parents was that I should have a station in life that was insulated from economic hardship—like being doctor. My job was to strive, labor, and push to the front to realize this dream.

So I grew up developing an aggressive achievement-oriented body. When challenged I go into achievement mode and plow in. I automatically enter into challenging situations energetically and aggressively, usually in a mood of mild anxiety. I have a sort of "let me at 'em so that I can prove myself" attitude. Friends, colleagues, and my family know this about me. In fact, when I'm really trying hard, I stick my tongue out, à la Michael Jordan. My children laughingly point this out to me. They have even captured this conditioned tendency in photos of me playing tennis or volleyball.

But there is more to my physical reactivity. I discovered this when I recently participated in a course on body awareness. The course instructor, Richard Heckler, wanted me and my fellow participants to perform in a centered and balanced way various exercises and routines drawn from the discipline of aikido. By centered and balanced, Richard meant without leaning forward or back and without shrinking toward the floor or rising in arrogance. He told us that aesthetically, mechanically, and functionally the movements proceeded best from "center."

My body wouldn't listen. It sensed the challenge of novelty, and as I performed each exercise, I automatically leaned, chin forward, into the movement, as if to prove that I could get it "right." As I tried harder, my tongue even stuck out in effort. In my unexamined eagerness, my body's center surged forward so that the heel of my back foot came off the floor. I became uncentered, off balance. Because of this, Richard nicknamed me "Chief Back-Foot-Down" to remind me of this automatic behavior. None of this was intentional for me; it simply happened.

Like Barbara, my physical response occurred *before* thought, i.e., automatically. Also like Barbara, my tendency has physical consequences. I carry a lot of tension in my back and neck, especially when I feel challenged. I don't wheeze like Barbara, and different circumstances trigger me, but this is my version of patterned reactivity.

We Are Biological Beings

So how does this triggering happen? The Barbara experience showed me that my traditional understanding of bodies was valuable but incomplete. I knew I needed to know more to be able to make "sense" of this experience. I needed new "eyes" of understanding to see not just Barbara, but this phenomenon in all people.

As a physician I had learned the sciences of the body: anatomy, physiology, biochemistry, etc. My medical training had also told me that the mind was governed by nonbody phenomena that seemed abstract, processes like denial, transference, projection, ego, and id. These actions of the mind were separate from physical consequences. The actions of the mind couldn't be touched, observed, and measured like those of a physical organ.

Here was my clinical dilemma—there was no intellectual bridge of understanding to connect Barbara's mind to her wheezing. Descartes ruled my world. The connection between thinking and the physical body is not absent, however, in other cultures. For example, Eastern disciplines like Buddhism often use the term *suffering* to refer to a state of uneasiness of thought and body simultaneously. People automatically fall into this state when their life's journey doesn't go as they think it should. In the Eastern view, suffering is not a mind state, but a state of the body and mind as one, a whole-person state.

In contrast, modern Western medicine addresses pain as a symptom that indicates that part of the body is not working or is injured. Pain is in the body; a doctor is trained to diagnose and manage it. Pain has quality, duration, location, and intensity. The whole person or any process that we call mental—like frustration, despair, fear—is not part of this view. Doctors do not ask "What does the pain mean for you?" "What is your experience with pain?" "What are your fears?" The Western medical perspective is based on understanding the parts of people. In this view, if you add up all of the parts and coordinate them, you get a whole being. When a part fails, it hurts and it must be fixed.

Obviously, you and I are more than the sum of our parts. We have unique cares, intentions, commitments, feelings, etc. We have preferences—love for our children, a passion for truth and learning, a curiosity about nature. And we suffer over things and people we want or have lost. None of this can be explained by examining our parts. We exist as whole and unique organisms. We are part of nature and nature is seamless, a connected whole. Only in our explanatory systems is it separated.

The Seamlessness of Nature

If we look at nature through our modern Western eyes, we see entities that appear to be separate and distinct. If we view nature through other eyes—the eyes of the Old Testament psalmist, or the stories that inspire native Americans—the world appears whole and seamless. More and more, cutting-edge advances in science, particularly in physics, demonstrate that all things are connected. In nature, separation is an illusion, not a reality. Like the mind-body split, the splits we see are a product of our thinking.

The seamless world exists right in front of our eyes. As I sit here in Maine writing this book, I can look out of the window and see grass, trees, sun, water, birds, and sky. To me they all look separate and distinct, and for our commonsense purposes they are. I can describe the birds to my wife, Roz. I can cut the grass. I can lie in the warmth of the sun. But, as I will show you, these things are all related. The problem of separateness is with me the perceiver, not with the objects perceived; I simply cannot see the connectedness.

When I change my perspective for just a moment, I see unity everywhere. The trees use energy from sunlight to produce cellulose and starch from the carbon dioxide in the air and water in the soil. The green pigment chlorophyll captures this energy and hands it over to the carbohydrate factory, i.e., cellulose and starch. The trees need cellulose to grow tall and capture more of the energy of the sun, and the starch for their own energy on cloudy days or at night when the sun isn't shining, a stored midnight snack.

As the trees capture energy and make carbohydrates, they release oxygen into the atmosphere. In fact, the oxygen in our atmosphere is entirely a product of living green things. This essential element for life emanates from plants that make starch and cellulose and in the process give off the very life-giving oxygen that we need for our existence. When I think like this I can see why environmentalists are concerned about the destruction of the rain forests. They see this destruction as potential suicide, because their view has been opened up enough to see that in this very special sense, they "are" the rain forests. Their claim is that these dense oxygen factories are essential for survival. Our lives are coupled with the trees in Brazil.

And of course it goes on. Animals, including you and me, get our energy not from the sun as plants do but by eating and burning stored plant starches in various forms. An alfalfa patch, a doughnut (from flour of plant origin), or a hamburger (the result of an animal using the starch to produce proteins) nourish us. But the nutrients have their origin in the interaction of green things with sunlight. Dunkin' Donuts, McDonald's, or the supermarket simply transport products of solar origin to our mouths.

Having ingested the starch or protein, we need to burn it for warmth and energy. To do this we need the very oxygen that was a by-product of the making of starch and cellulose by plants. The oxidation of the starch releases the stored energy derived from the sun.

As we animals burn the starch, carbon dioxide is produced. This carbon dioxide is the raw material that our plant partners use along with solar energy to make oxygen and starch in the first place. We're all connected in a cosmic cycle, and this is only the tiniest part of it. What a miracle—a seamless unity.

And to our eyes it looks like birds, trees, sky, sun—all separate.

In nature there is one cycle of intimate relatedness. For my eyes there are only separate parts and things. In fact, we've created dozens of disciplines within science to explore each separate thing or class of things. We have plant scientists, who are called botanists. Students of animal life are called zoologists. Others study rocks and are called geologists. Our mind breaks things apart to achieve understanding.

The fruits of this scientific understanding are tremendous. This is nowhere more evident than in medicine. We can understand parts magnificently and generate valuable information. But our very process of breaking apart for the sake of understanding blinds us to a deeper truth about life—its seamlessness, its unity, its total interdependence.

The Man in the Five-Foot Scarf

The next germinal moment in my seeing the possibility of a new approach to medicine came nearly fifteen years ago. I was at Harvard's

Cronkhite Graduate Center, attending an all-day seminar with the intriguing title "Language, Biology, and the Nature of Life." The seminar leaders were two Chileans. One was a philosopher, Fernando Flores, who later became one of my most valued teachers. Fernando has made important contributions to our understanding of language, culture, learning, and entrepreneurship, and I'll have more to say about him in chapter 4. The other presenter was the biologist Humberto Maturana.

For a university as prestigious and conservative as Harvard, Maturana presented an unconventional, even shocking appearance. He had long, disheveled graying hair, a bushy mustache, round glasses that framed eyes that burned with passion and wit, and a five-foot-long woolen scarf that wound around his neck, its ends flailing in the air like uncoordinated wings. He never took off his scarf despite the warmth of the seminar room. His carefully designed iconoclastic image foretold the content of his message.

With brilliance and unarguable logic, Maturana built over three continuous hours a rigorous, scientifically incontrovertible argument that literally changed how I thought about living things, humans included.

After years of studying biological evolution (how we came to be) and experimental neuroscience (how nerves and brains work), Maturana reached two important conclusions. They may seem simplistic at first glance, but they are, in fact, very deep in their implications.

Maturana's first conclusion is that *all living systems are closed systems.* What this means in everyday terms is that you, me, and all living beings, even a simple single-celled organism, respond to environmental events in a way that reflects their internal structure. To put it another way, the behavior of living things is not dictated by the environment, but is a reflection of their internal structure activated by the environment.

For example, some bacteria have the structural capability to eat certain sugars; others do not. If a scientist places a sugar-eating bacterium near a trough of sugar, it moves toward the sugar, triggered by its presence. If a scientist puts a non-sugar-eating bacterium in the same environment, it doesn't move toward the sugar. It's not triggered by the presence of sugar; its structure does not allow it to be triggered. We say it doesn't want the sugar.

This is a profoundly radical idea. When I first heard it, I couldn't fully grasp its meaning. It may be the same for you. I felt like the people who first heard Christopher Columbus's thinking about the earth's shape, or Freud's notion of the unconscious. These ideas didn't fit the frame of understanding that they lived in and left people baffled, confused, upset, or intolerant of the novel claims.

Sitting in the lecture hall, I wondered: How could the environment not instruct us? Is life simply a reflection of our structure? The best way for you to deal with this biological truth at this moment is not to try to refute it or totally understand it. Just try to dwell with it, like a big question—Could this be so? I will return to this notion many times. It will become clearer as you do the various exercises in the book.

As Maturana continued his argument, he proposed that people are like machines in regards to our relationship with the environment. A machine is a thing designed to perform a specific set of tasks. Its parts are designed and organized to do that job. When activated, the machine does the job that its structure is designed to do. For instance, when I start my lawnmower, it doesn't make coffee, it cuts grass. It does what its structure allows it to do when I pull on its cord.

An external trigger (an event in the environment like pulling the cord) doesn't change the machine, it *activates* it. My car key doesn't cause the engine to start. Rather, it triggers a set of parts that constitute the machine's structure. My pulling the lawnmower's cord doesn't tell the machine to get ready to cut grass. Instead, it activates the mechanism designed and organized to cut grass.

Walter, the Angry Man

Walter grew angry when I claimed that people resemble machines. "Who are you calling a machine?" he snapped.

I replied, "I'm not talking about you in particular, but about all living systems. Since we are living, biological systems, I suggest that you listen to what I'm saying and see if it applies to you."

Walter roared back, saying, "I see where this is going and I don't like it! You're going to blame me, not the jerks around me."

I urged him to look at whether he was triggered from time to time.

He answered before I finished speaking: "Only by jerks!"

When you think about your life and Maturana's first conclusion, as Walter did, what do you see for yourself? Whatever it is, it arises from and lives within your structure and is triggered by events in your life.

You instinctively know how a car or lawnmower starts, though I doubt that you have ever thought of it in the way I described it. Your actions with lawnmowers and cars are consistent with your understanding of how a machine functions. If you turn the key and the car doesn't start, you don't go to a locksmith for a new key or to an orthopedic doctor to examine your arm. The car not starting implies that something in its structure is out of whack. And, since the car isn't a living system with self-healing capabilities, you take it to an auto mechanic for repairs.

Maturana's claim was that not only do machines work this way, but that living systems work this way as well. The behaviors elicited by the environment are determined by the structure of the living thing. The environment releases, or calls forth, these behaviors, but does not determine them. The environment is like the starter key, we are like the car. Maturana gave the name *structural determinism* to this notion.

Gretchen, the Perfectionist

In class, Gretchen raised her hand and said, "Sometimes, when my boss gives me a tough assignment, my chest gets tight and my stomach growls. Is this what you mean?"

I answered that people have patterned reactions to environmental triggers and this may be what happens for her. I suggested that she keep looking at her responses because she was on the right track.

The Frog with the Rotated Eye

Maturana cited one of his own experiments—the "Frog with the Rotated Eye"—to support his claim that all living things are closed, structure-determined systems.

At an early stage of a frog's development, Maturana surgically rotated one of its eyes 180 degrees without damaging the frog or its eye. However, the frog's structure had now been altered, and it acted consistent with its new structure.

When Maturana covered the frog's normal eye, the frog could only see with its rotated eye. This caused visual images that normally fall on one side of the frog's retina, the light-sensitive tissue at the back of the eye, to land 180 degrees away on the other side of the retina. When that occurred, unusual things happened to the frog's behavior.

Normally, if a fly showed up in the frog's field of vision, it would shoot out its tongue to catch the fly—lunch. But because of the change in its eye, the frog shot out its tongue 180 degrees away from where the fly was—no lunch. The frog's actions were consistent with its structure, but wrong for catching the fly.

In Maturana's terms, the environment triggered the frog to respond; the response was a manifestation of the frog's altered structure. Without the good eye, this would be one very hungry, frustrated frog! Fortunately for the frog, it learned an effective behavior with time and practice and finally could catch flies despite its altered structure.

Like the frog, all living things act in a structurally determined way. Barbara's asthma, her feeling of anger, her sweaty palms, her thoughts of aggression toward the course leader were all internally consistent, highly interdependent, structurally determined events. The environment did not *cause* Barbara to experience this sequence of bodily events; rather, it *triggered* her structurally determined system. (I like the term *trigger,* because a trigger does not shoot a bullet, it releases something in the mechanism of the gun that fires bullets.)

Remember, no one else in the seminar had Barbara's response. My response was an urgent desire to help Barbara; it arose out of my structure altered to be a physician. The elements for firing Barbara's asthmatic response were already in her body. They were present when she walked into the room, even before the course leader appeared. She was an asthma attack waiting to happen.

Perception Is Structurally Determined

After Maturana had shaken my scientific worldview, i.e., that we take information in, with his first observation, he rocked me again with his second observation about what it is to know something.

In his view, perception (seeing) does not involve taking in an event or thing; analyzing or trying to understand it (knowing); and then acting accordingly. Rather, perception and knowing are not representations of reality; they are a *reflection in action* of what you as a mechanism see, understand, or do. In short, *perception is structurally determined.*

What does Maturana mean by this phrase? An easy way to grasp what he's saying is to imagine for a moment that you are a fifteenth-century Italian. At that time, you lived in a culture that believed that the earth was flat. If you stood on a beach in Genoa and watched a sailboat adventurously sail off into the distance, getting smaller and smaller, what would happen? If you had a friend on the boat, you'd panic because you'd perceive that the boat would fall off the edge of the earth and that your friend would perish.

Your perception is real enough to you, as your sweaty palms would indicate. What you wouldn't see is that your perception is the result of the flat-earth common sense of the time embodied in your structure. Your structure would act consistent with your beliefs.

A modern example reinforces the point. Do you love to watch sunsets? I do. Poems, songs, romance, peaceful endings to summer days of joy—all of this comes up for me at sunset. The only problem with this is that for four hundred years we have known that the sun does not set. It stays where it is, the earth turns. Yet the next time you see a sunset, I guarantee that you will see it set. Your old romantic structure tells you so.

Robert, the High Achiever

At this point in the classroom discussion, Robert raised his hand and asked for some references to read about what I was saying. I told him that I would give him some after the class, but I asked why he wanted them.

Robert replied, "I want to learn the course material. Reading and studying it at home would help me."

I suggested this was not "school" material where he learned "about" things. This was a different kind of learning. I advised him to "keep listening, ask questions, and trust me to teach you."

Robert said, "I hate the state of confusion that I'm in. The uncertainty of this kind of learning makes me uneasy." I asked him a question not for an answer, but to invite his reflection: "How come not having the answer makes you uneasy?"

He grew quiet and sat back in his chair, thinking about what I had said.

To tell the truth, I too was uneasy when Maturana confronted me with this fact. You may find yourself having similar feelings at this moment. Again, my advice is to sit with it, or observe fully whatever feelings come up for you.

Listening to Maturana's lecture for me was like my childhood encounter with Minnie. I knew I was hearing something important, even if I didn't fully understand it. I was at a point in my learning where I was about to take Robert Frost's famed road "less traveled by, and that has made all of the difference."

The implications of Maturana's teachings are tremendous. First, if you want to change yourself, you have to change your structurally determined responses, not alter your environment. Our tendencies to blame others or play the victim are threatened.

Second, if your responses are determined by your structure, and if your structure is developed in your past, then at any given moment you are doing only and exactly what your past allows. This gave me a biological basis for compassion and respect for myself and others. We are doing only what we can do, given our history.

As I sat there in the Cronkhite Center, thoughts shot through my head like fireworks on the Fourth of July. So much of what Maturana was saying was true to my experience, but something bothered me deeply. Was I, were all of us like machines, merely mechanisms waiting to be set in motion? Are we victims of our biological selves?

Intuitively I knew this was not true. Picasso, Galileo, Louis Armstrong, Katharine Hepburn were not machines limited by their structures. Invention, love, creativity, learning are all part of life. So given Maturana's views, how is change possible? The key, as you will learn later in this chapter, has to do with certain properties of the brain itself. It is plastic, by which I mean that its very structure can be altered through experience. In fact, the biological basis of all learning is structural change.

So you are not condemned to repeat the same actions forever, as my encounter with a village chief in Togo proved.

The Togo Chief

In light of Maturana's notion of structurally determined patterns, my meeting with a village chief from the country of Togo took on an entirely different meaning.

In the early 1970s, the World Health Organization (WHO) was determined to eliminate smallpox globally. At that time, smallpox was an international scourge, but one amenable to medical intervention. It was clear that the body's response (structurally determined) to the smallpox virus is either to become very ill and recover, thereby eliminating the virus from the body, or to die. If all people could be vaccinated (a structural change that makes a person immune to actual infection), the virus would have no place to go and would eventually disappear. There are no known animal hosts or hiding places for the smallpox virus. Armed with this knowledge, WHO embarked on a major vaccination effort for the global eradication of smallpox. I was a team leader responsible for some preliminary work in the country of Togo, which is where I met the chief.

It was mid-morning on an excruciatingly hot day in West Africa when our team reached the tiny remote village of Tschamba. Although well off the beaten track and unmapped, we had heard about Tschamba from the people of neighboring villages. As our Land Rover inched up the dry riverbed toward the center of town, the villagers' faces showed curiosity and fear. Rarely had they had contact with the outside world.

We had learned from experience that our first stop when visiting a village must be with the chief, who was typically the administrative and religious leader. To secure his blessings for our vaccination project, we'd bring him a gift. Bob Scholtens, an epidemiologist on our team, had had the brilliant idea of taking a Polaroid camera along with us and presenting each chief with his photo.

For two months, the gift of a photo had worked like a charm. We'd meet the village chief, and after appropriate greetings and presenting a letter from the Togo Ministry of Health, we'd snap his picture. A minute later we'd present the gift to him. Uniformly the chiefs were thrilled. They always reciprocated by assisting us in our task—calling the village together, lining up the children, etc.

This day, however, was different. After our interpreter, Saliou, asked to see the chief, we were whisked to his small, thatched-roof house. The chief was striking looking—tall, with a white beard, white hair, and wearing a white turban and a red velvet cape. After we exchanged greetings, I took the chief's photo and when it had developed, handed it to him. The chief had no visible reaction and gave it back to me. I thought, "He didn't like the photo. Maybe it wasn't his best side." So I changed positions and took another photo. Again, he handed it back to me. After a third, then fourth attempt I realized something was seriously wrong.

I was beginning to get uneasy. I felt slightly fearful. I asked Saliou for an explanation. He replied, "I don't think he knows what this is! He does not see the photo of him." That seemed impossible. After a short and uncomfortable pause, Saliou got out of his chair and led the chief to the edge of a riverbank that was about ninety feet away.

Here, Saliou asked the chief to lean over and look at his reflection in the water. Then he held a photo between the chief and the reflection. The chief seemed irritated and confused. "What is going on with these people?" his body language said. "First they put pieces of paper in front of me, then they have me bend over my river. These Americans are very curious." Saliou persisted. All at once the chief let out a resounding "Ahhhh!" and proceeded to laugh for what seemed like an eternity.

The chief apparently had finally seen that his water reflection was present on the paper! It was like magic for him—"How did I get onto the paper?" he said with a mixture of excitement and wonder. Then he insisted that we take more photos of him and of his entire family before beginning our work.

As I sat in the audience at the Cronkhite Center I now had a biological explanation for the amazing moment with the chief, far better than Saliou's "I don't think he knows what this is!" The chief's structure, his brain and nervous system, had not been changed by living with photos. Photographs—certainly not instant ones—were not part of his reality. A photo would trigger in each one of us a socially consistent form of behavior. The chief's structure produced a very different reaction; he reacted as if to an annoying colored piece of paper and persistent strangers shoving it in front of him. The chief was literally blind to the photo as a likeness of him. Psychologists call this condition *cognitive blindness*.

Linda, the Depressed Woman

After hearing this story, Linda blurted out, "I'm trapped and my life is hopeless. I have no work that I like to do, my children are grown, and my husband works all the time. I don't have any future." She said this with the certainty that she was describing something real.

I said to her, "I don't know your future any more than you do. But I asked you to reflect on the chief's story. What would the chief have said if an instant photo were described to him before he had seen it? I mean, really *seen* it?"

Linda replied, "He would have probably said that it was impossible." I agreed and said that life's like that. "We can't see what we can't see. Maybe there are possibilities for your life that you haven't seen yet."

Linda said that she doubted it.

"What if you're wrong?" I asked.

Linda became thoughtful and said, "Then I'd be wasting my life, wouldn't I?" Her mood lifted slightly as she smiled. Then she quickly returned to looking depressed and a bit agitated.

Cognitive blindness: We simply do not see what we do not see. That is not to say we don't see shapes, colors, light and dark, etc. But we don't see meaning and context unless living and learning has modified our structures. Maturana calls this *structural coupling.*

Such learning happens from immersion in a social context, a culture. The chief had no exposure to photos and especially instant photos. But he did have experience with his reflection in the water. Only by making the connection could he see his likeness on the photographic paper. And only then did the Polaroid box become for him a box for making likenesses without water.

As I sat half listening to Maturana conclude his remarks, I knew that the seeds were planted in me for a new understanding about living things, about Barbara, about my patients, about myself, and about learning and change. I began to ask myself how my patients' structurally determined tendencies shaped their lives, generated their symptoms, and altered the course of their diseases. More importantly, how could such insights be translated into creating new minds and building new bodies?

As I continued my search for understanding after Maturana's lecture, I discovered new research on the brain that not only provided evidence for Maturana's theories, but also gave a solid scientific basis for habits, cognitive blindness, and change and learning.

The Biology of the Remembered Present

The brain is, in large part, what makes us human.

Three biological aspects make the brain unique. First, it is composed of billions and billions of cells; second, each individual cell has innumerable connections, which generate countless combinations and configurations. The brain is thus capable of tremendous variety, change, and novelty. And third, the brain is plastic, able to "rewire" itself into new structural configurations in response to life's experiences. When it does, new structures are generated. Subsequent life events can trigger this altered brain, and a new response appears. This is a simple explanation of the biological basis of learning.

How the brain does this restructuring is a major focus of neuroscience. A leader in this field is Gerald Edelman, director of the Neurosciences Institute and chairman of the Department of Neurobiology at the Scripps Research Institute. Edelman has been interested for years in how the experiences of living things alters their structures so that subsequent responses are changed. In short, he wants to know how living systems learn.

Edelman's early research was not on the nervous system but on the immune system. The immune system is that group of the body's cells and organs that is altered by exposure to infection or immunization. This system alters its structure from its "experience" so that it can take new action. In this case, that new action is the production of specific antibodies against dangerous infection. This is called *acquired resistance*—a kind of body learning that is structurally based. It was to produce this acquired resistance through immunization that I had traveled to Africa.

For instance, people who have had measles generally do not get it a second time; people who have had polio immunizations do not get polio; and people like the vaccinated villagers in Togo do not come down with smallpox. In all these cases, people's structures have been intentionally altered so that they recognize and neutralize the virus. Such experience-altered bodies are fortified by cells that have learned to fight a specific challenge. Edelman explored how the immune system "learns" and published a series of studies in the 1960s and 1970s for which he was awarded the Nobel Prize.

Bright Air, Brilliant Fire

For the last twenty years, Edelman has been studying how the brain changes with experience. He wrote a popular account of his findings in 1992 called *Bright Air, Brilliant Fire: On the Matter of the Mind.* In his book, he pointed to three aspects of the brain that account for its remarkable ability to generate both stability (repetition of function) and novelty (new structurally based function or learning).

The first aspect is that of genetics, or what we inherit that equips us to live as humans. We have a structure in common with other human beings that allows us to speak, to walk on our hind legs, etc. This basic set of functions is shared by members of the species, but also has inherited constraints. I will never be a Tiger Woods, Mozart, or Maria Callas, but I share many functions with them. Edelman calls this basic set the *primary repertoire.* My primary repertoire is my starting point, my genetic inheritance, the building blocks in my kit.

The second property he describes as follows: "During life, the connections of nerve cells are selectively strengthened or weakened by biochemical and physical processes. With recurrence a new 'anatomical network of function' is carved out of the primary repertoire."

This is the learned or *secondary repertoire.* Like my mother used to say, if I practice the piano daily, I'll learn how to play. Edelman would say that my mother was asking me to develop a new secondary repertoire in my body that, when triggered by the black marks on the page, would lead to actions that my teacher could recognize as passable Mozart.

But learning is not function specific. What I mean by this is that if I learn that certain species of snakes are dangerous, then when I see one a complex array of behaviors is triggered in some sequence or other: my heartbeat quickens, I move quickly in the opposite direction, the emotion of fear arises, and I say, "That's a rattlesnake." These functions—control of heartbeat, movements, emotions, and thoughts—are anatomically situated in different parts of the brain. How do they all get activated simultaneously in a coordinated response? Edelman proposes that different parts of the brain connect and coordinate with one another through a process called *reentry.* Certain reentrant patterns become strengthened between different parts of the brain to produce complex behavioral responses. Barbara's reactions involved many systems in her body reacting in a coordinated way.

This may seem like heavy stuff, but it can be summarized simply—your behavior is structurally determined, and you can learn to alter your structure.

Gretchen, the Perfectionist

"All of this information about learning and how the brain changes is interesting, but learning is very hard for me. I get so nervous," Gretchen said.

I asked her if this was always so and she replied, "Yes."

"Are you afraid of learning?" I asked.

She responded by saying that wasn't exactly it, but learning made her nervous nonetheless. "That's why I never went on in school," Gretchen said with a note of remorse.

I asked her to live with this question: "What about learning makes you anxious and frightened?" She said that she would.

Memory Is Not Just in the Brain

Richard Heckler, the instructor mentioned at the beginning of this chapter who labeled me Chief Back-Foot-Down, is a remarkable teacher who brings several traditions to his work. (By my structural definition, a culture or tradition is kept alive by a group of people who share the same explanations and activities about something and whose structures have been modified in a similar way.)

Richard is trained in psychology—the analysis and treatment of mental functions. He is also highly accomplished in aikido, a martial art. As a practitioner of this tradition, he is deeply aware of body states and postures. The state of your body in life, at any moment, determines your possibilities and barriers for action.

As an aikido teacher, Richard observes the automatic tendencies of students that keep them from performing the practice in a centered and effective way. It was Richard who saw my automatic, structurally determined tendency to rush in, to be aggressively off center.

In his book *The Anatomy of Change,* Richard makes the following point: "In the course of our development we make certain choices to survive. These choices often involve dealing with fear, anger, embarrassment, etc., by some armoring or automatic behavior that assures survival."

For example, a person who has been deeply embarrassed as a child may manifest an array of automatic behaviors that serve to avoid embarrassment. She'll sit in the back row at school, wear subdued clothing, never volunteer for a solo performance, etc.—all unconscious actions, but patterned. In addition, her shoulders may be stooped, her voice soft, and her face expressionless as she hides her emotions from what she feels is the watching and dangerous world.

Such a person avoids fear and anxiety-provoking situations with a set of somatic behavioral and emotional responses that Richard calls her *conditioned tendency.* He writes, "It is a way of being we assume when we believe that on some level our identity is threatened; our muscles set in a particular way. We assume a certain posture, breathe a certain way, take a stance that literally manifests that tendency. This tendency, which is actually imprinted in the flesh by many years of use, takes over, and we lose touch with the present moment."

Walter, the Angry Man

As I read Richard's words in class, Walter became angry, saying, "What do you mean, 'takes over'? Nothing and nobody takes me over. I'm in control of my life and you aren't going to tell me otherwise with this scientific crap."

As he said this, his face reddened, the veins of his neck bulged, his voice became louder, and his fists clenched. The rest of the people in the room had their own automatic bodily reactions to Walter's rage.

I had to take a deep breath to keep myself from being "taken over" by my automatic reaction to Walter's anger. As I did, I had a sudden flash of compassion for his wife. When I had composed myself, I told him that, in my opinion, his kind of taking care of himself has a very high cost.

"That's what you say," he responded almost before I was finished, "but no one else can do the job better than I can."

We are miraculously blessed creatures, but creatures nonetheless. As such we are governed by biological principles. In this chapter I have shown that one such principle is that your structure determines your reactions to the environment—what you see, do, feel, and think.

But how did you get the structure you have? And, can you change it? These were burning questions for me and must be so for you.

EXERCISES

Major Points in Chapter 2

□ The behavior of living systems is structurally determined. In this way they are similar to machines. A machine's function is determined by its structure, i.e., it does what its structure allows it to do by design. Living systems, including people, share this same property.

□ What you experience, feel, and perceive is determined by your structure and is *triggered* by the environment. An external event is like a car's ignition key—it doesn't determine what the car does, it only activates its structure.

□ Perception—what you see—is not "reality," but rather what your structure can and does see. The story of the Togo chief illustrates this phenomenon. His history had not produced a structure that recognized a photo. Hence he was "blind" to it.

□ In human beings, the brain is the central organ for learning. Its natural structure has the property of plasticity, i.e., it can change through recurrent experience. When the brain has been altered by experience and is then triggered by the environment, it acts differently than it did before the "learning."

□ The brain's structure at any moment is a product of its natural inheritance and the summation of all of the structural modifications that have occurred during the course of its life.

□ The human brain is unique in the animal kingdom because it has the innate capacity to generate language. This gives us the possibility of designing our future, not just extending the past. We'll discuss this in later chapters.

A Brief Check on Previous Learning

In chapter 1's exercise section you explored your learning style. What reactions did you have to a learning situation? What emotions came up for you in learning?

As you move along in the exercises, carry chapter 1's practices forward. Keep observing yourself as a learner. I suggest that you take time each week to review your "findings" from the previous workbook sessions, just for a few minutes. Such a practice-review-practice sequence will facilitate your learning.

The Awareness Exercise

By now you should have begun regular meditation. How is it going for you? Notice if you're having trouble doing this exercise regularly. Do you sometimes have difficulty following through on other resolutions that you make to yourself? If so, become aware of that tendency. Remember, this is the awareness exercise; use everything that happens to increase your self-awareness. When I began meditating, it was difficult to sit still for ten minutes. Are you having this problem?

Do you face other barriers to meditation? For me it was a lack of time. It still is. When this happens I have two choices: let staying fully "booked" run my life and generate excuses, or recognize an old conversation and recommit to learning. When I told my meditation teacher of my time pressure he said, "Create more time by getting up earlier."

"Am I doing it right?" is a common concern of my patients. I have two answers. First, reread the instructions and follow them—that's it! There is no right way or wrong way to meditate. After a while, you'll stop trying to understand the instructions and just do them. Second, reflect on why you're raising this question. Does it come up often for you in other areas? Are you afraid of doing things the wrong way? Are you a doing-it-right junkie?

Whatever problems you're facing, keep on observing yourself and keep on meditating.

Automatic Writing

In chapter 1's exercise section, you learned about automatic writing. Now, let's do automatic writing on automatic writing.

Write for three minutes on what you think you can learn from automatic writing. Include your attitude toward the activity and any emotions or moods that come up for you. Include your speculations on what automatic writing is and why we include it here.

Write continuously; don't let your pen stop moving. Even if you have nothing to say, keep writing.

Automatic Writing

What did you observe about yourself in this exercise about writing and about thinking itself? About your reactions? I remember when I first did this exercise, it was painful for me to force myself to write before I thought out what to write. My tendency to "do it right" came to the fore.

Exercises for Reflection and Learning

The following exercises help you observe that your body changes from moment to moment because of different triggerings during the day. In these exercises you'll observe the "whole body" reactions of your structure and those of others.

Body awareness is not a cultural strength of those of us in the Western world. In fact, the opposite is true. We put tremendous emphasis on reason at the expense of intuition and body listening. But body awareness is an important skill to learn because it is a fundamental component of what is called *emotional intelligence*.

Your body is the manifestation at this very moment of millions and millions of years of evolution. You are a miracle of creation and evolution. Your body is precious, infinitely complex, and brilliantly sensitive to environmental triggers. It is the vehicle of your awareness, of your creativity, of your dignity, and of your love. But you, like most of us, rarely look at it or pay attention to it.

Observing Your Body—Exercise One: The Mirror Exercise

To increase your body awareness, stand in your underwear—or au naturel—in front of a full-length or large mirror for three minutes. Notice whatever judgments or thoughts come up for you automatically.

Be aware of positive judgments like gratitude, admiration, or love. Recognize negative judgments like "I'm too fat" or "My hips are too big." Note changes that habits like sports, physical labor, or eating too much have produced in your body. Notice the impact of age on your body. See if you can appreciate the miracle of your body and your gift of life. Keep looking for three full minutes even if this makes you uncomfortable.

Pay attention to the emotions that occur in connection with your thoughts. What do you see here about the connection between your judgments and the state of your body?

Look at your face, your expression, a smile that you may nervously make, lines, wrinkles, etc. Notice how your body is etched by life.

Take notes on your reflections for use later with your automatic writing.

Notes
(Observing Your Body—Exercise One)

Observing Your Body—Exercise Two: The Daily Event Exercise

For this exercise you need to carry a small pad of paper or use your portable computer organizer.

The daily event exercise helps you observe in detail the ways in which your body is triggered and changes during the course of a day.

With each major daily event—an argument with your spouse, your child bringing home a report card, your attending a meeting, a phone call from an old friend—notice your body's reaction. Pay special attention to those situations that "touch" you, in both good and bad ways. Take notes on the pad of paper you're carrying with you or on your computer organizer.

In the course of a day, you may observe tightening of certain muscle groups in places like your shoulders, your neck, your forehead, or your back. Or you may notice your heart pounding or your palms sweating. Some people when they are triggered have sensations in their belly. Others reach for a cigarette or a snack.

> ☐ *Recently, I noticed that after a particularly stressful day I went to the refrigerator for a late-night snack. I had been doing this for years. I realized that I have "my wires crossed." What I should be doing is going to sleep when I feel exhausted. Instead, I was ignoring my body's good sense.*

A patient of mine named Eva, a twenty-nine-year-old business consultant, also suffered from a lack of body awareness. Eva was referred to the program because of anxiety attacks. She told me that in the past she had only noticed her anxiety when the attacks almost made her lose consciousness.

After doing this exercise, Eva began to recognize that the anxiety attacks occurred in mild form often each day. She noticed the sweaty palms, the pounding heart, and the shortness of breath in their incipient or early forms. When she began to notice these early warning signs, sometimes she was able to "be with" the symptoms or use deep breathing to abort the attacks.

How old is the pattern of reaction that you are noting in your body? What is its history? What are the stories about your life that you connect with your reaction(s)?

For example, here is what one patient wrote in his notes:

Jordan broke a promise to call me. It made me angry and righteous. I said to myself, "I don't forget my promises, why do you forget yours?" A tightness developed in the back of my neck. I recalled long periods of time when I had neck pain. The question that I asked myself is how does a friend's breaking his word cause my neck to hurt?

Another patient wrote in his notes:

I've lived the life of a creative loner. I'm my own person, I make my own rules. Recently, I've fallen in love with a woman called Rebecca. When I see her I become afraid. On the one hand, I want to be intimate with Rebecca. On the other hand, I've made many sacrifices to build a life that I like. Trying to decide what to do has given me insomnia. What am I afraid of? Why does this fear make it impossible for me to go to sleep?

Look for patterns in your body reactions to daily events. Are there reactions associated with anger, with joy, with anxiety, with frustration, etc.? Are there reactions to certain kinds of events like a broken promise, or someone making a request of you, or having to place your trust in someone?

Make notes below for your automatic writing, which you'll do to conclude this chapter's exercises.

Notes
(Observing Your Body—Exercise Two)

Observing Your Body—Exercise Three: The Music Exercise

Music is more than meets the ears. It provides a mood-altering experience that changes the entire body. Moreover, it is the expression in sound of a people or of a culture. The bodies of members of that culture, whether Hispanic, Chinese, Generation X, African-American, are "tuned"—structurally altered—to move with their music. Think about being depressed while dancing to Tito Puente—very difficult; conversely, try to party with Mahler playing in the background.

For this exercise, go to a room where you have a radio, or, for convenience, use your car radio. First, pick a station that plays music that you like and are familiar with. If you're at home, sit in a chair, close your eyes, and listen to the music. If you're driving, pull over to a rest spot and listen to the music.

Do this with your whole body. Allow your body to be moved by the music. Move your head, shake your shoulders, tap your feet. Just let it happen. Enjoy this for several minutes.

Now tune to a station that has music that you generally do not listen to—ethnic, rap, classical, country, etc.—and repeat the exercise. Again, listen with your whole body. Observe your response. Does your body want to move in rhythm with the music, or does it withdraw and shut down, feel awkward or uncomfortable, etc.?

Remember this is someone else's music. It moves them.

Try this with several different radio stations.

This exercise has many purposes. First, you're building your body awareness in different circumstances. Second, you can become aware that your body is tuned by your history and culture to react to different experiences. Third, it gives you some awareness of your body, which will help you build relationships with others whose bodies are tuned differently from yours. By this I mean you can either feel uncomfortable or awkward with people who live and enjoy music that is different from music that you like, or you can learn to tolerate your natural discomfort and listen to their music—to them, really. There is no "right" music, just different music.

Take notes on what you observed for use in automatic writing later on.

Notes
(Observing Your Body—Exercise Three)

Observing Your Body—Exercise Four: Observing the Bodies of Others

This exercise should be a lot of fun. I want you to pretend to be Sherlock Holmes when you observe the bodies of others. Remember how Holmes would astonish Dr. Watson by presenting a detailed portrait of a person from a few observations? "Elementary, my dear Watson," Holmes would reply when Watson asked how he could be so accurate with such little information. To the great detective, insights about others had become second nature. That is where you're headed.

Here are some "clues" to look for when observing people:

□ You can tell a great deal about people by their body posture. Is it centered or leaning either forward aggressively or back in embarrassment and withdrawal?

□ You can observe someone's walk. Is it tentative, belligerent, cool, relaxed, tense, or embarrassed?

□ You can also examine someone's facial expression. Does it show fear, joy, anxiety, resignation, deep concern? What can you see about a person's mood in his or her face?

□ Other questions to explore include: Are their movements stiff and restricted, or free and responsive? Is their speech pedantic, tentative, or firmly assertive? Are their hands fidgety or relaxed?

I once took a course at the Harvard Medical School from one of its great teachers, Dr. Walter Bauer. On morning rounds at Massachusetts General Hospital, he would spend an eternity, or so it seemed to me, talking about a patient's hands—the strength of the hands, the hygiene of the nails, the color of the skin. From his observations he could tell many things—how ill the patient was, how he or she made a living, his or her mood—all without laboratory tests, just by looking closely.

Focus, as Dr. Bauer did, on two or three strangers during a day. Do this in some way so as not to embarrass them or yourself. Make your observations and in private, even imitate their posture and facial expressions to feel what it may be like to be them.

In the space below, or in your journal or computer, write down your observations. Then make up a brief story of this person that describes the main features of his or her life based on the outline I give you below. Remember, this story is not the "truth," just what you make up as you play Sherlock Holmes.

Sample Notes

Name: Jack

Where did you meet him?: I met him briefly at a bar.

Posture: Slouched down, shoulders hung forward

Walk: Tentative

Speech: Thoughtful, unanimated, never emotional, precise

Mood the person is in: Mild depression

How the world looks to this person: Confusing, beating him down, almost hopeless, but still trying to figure it out

Brief life story for person number one: This is a bad time for Jack. His old plans, hopes, and dreams, his precise map for life has been upset and he is lost, almost in despair. He is not taking care of his body and has little to give to others.

Notes on Your Observations

Person number one

Name:

Where did you meet him/her?:

Posture:

Walk:

Speech:

Mood the person is in:

How the world looks to this person:

Brief life story for person number one:

Person number two

Name:

Where did you meet him/her?:

Posture:

Walk:

Speech:

Mood the person is in:

How the world looks to this person:

Brief life story for person number two:

What did you see in this exercise about the connection between bodies, behavior, and history? Do you think that you could learn to be as clever as Holmes? Take notes for the automatic writing later on.

Notes

Conclusion

In this chapter, you have begun to develop your skill at observing your own body and the bodies of others. The body that you see is the result of a person's life and, in turn, it is the very body that shapes the person's present-day experience.

Refer to your notes on the preceding "observe your body" exercises. Then write automatically about *it* and what you observed—how it reacts to joy, stress, learning, and new situations. What do you see about your body's reactions and your health? What do you see about your reactions and your history? Write for three minutes.

Automatic Writing

The Experiences of My Patients in Doing These Exercises

Gretchen, the Perfectionist

Gretchen had great difficulty with the exercises involving observing her body. "In my parents' religion, the body is seen as sinful. I try to never look at myself or the bodies of others. It was very difficult at first, but as I persisted, it became easier. I got to like my body a little."

In addition, Gretchen thought emotions were a sign of weakness. Her mother used to say, "Don't be childish!" whenever Gretchen would get upset. Gretchen had never learned to observe and identify the nuances of her own emotional life.

Gretchen was more successful in observing the emotions of others. She wondered why she couldn't read her own.

"You've practiced not doing that for thirty-five years," I suggested. "Maybe you can learn now if you want to."

She found it difficult to imitate others. In class, Gretchen was able to mimic a young woman who had walked by her apartment building the night before. This woman was attractive, walked with an easy grace, and had a soft, welcoming air about her. Gretchen said that the young woman looked as if she lived "trying to take everything in." She added, "This felt very strange to me, to be so open and relaxed—but it felt good."

I asked her what she thought it would take to be in the stranger's body style more of the time. "Good question," she answered, and began to think about it.

Walter, the Angry Man

At first, Walter said that he had seen "nothing" when he looked into the mirror. But when I pressed him, he replied that looking at his body made him sad. "I've beaten myself up pretty good. You know—smoking, drinking."

Regarding his observations, Walter said he saw one man with a furrowed brow, a jutting chin, and a stiff military walk. In class, when Walter put his body in this posture, he said, "It feels real familiar. I'm like that."

As I watched Walter's mimicry, I said, "You do that well because you've been practicing for forty-six years. Do you think that this body is a healthy body?" I asked, imitating his stance.

Walter stared at me thoughtfully but didn't reply.

After class, I gave him a copy of *Anger Kills* by Redford Williams and suggested that he read it. I wanted Walter to understand how his automatic body reactions were putting his heart and his very life in jeopardy.

Robert, the High Achiever

Robert said that he normally wasn't aware of other people's bodies. He added that he only paid attention to his body when he didn't feel well. In fact, Robert remarked that he never gave more than a momentary glance at his body. It was of no interest to him.

He explained that in his culture of Judaism, intelligence and education, not physical prowess, were the keys to success. No one in his family played sports or exercised. Physical work of any kind was disdained. "We should be able to be a big success with our brains," Robert said.

Robert listened to reggae music for exercise three. He said that it bothered him because it was "not real music" like Bach or Beethoven.

I pointed out that millions of people danced to that music. How could it not be real?

He was puzzled by my question. It looked "true" to him that only his approved music was "real" music. He lived automatically in this prejudice.

Robert's observation of another person involved a judge in a courtroom. The judge's manner was distinguished, attentive, and competent. His face radiated intelligence and confidence as he conducted the trial.

Robert said, "I have the hardest time showing dignity and confidence. I would be scared to death if I were a judge. I might make mistakes and my cases might be appealed. I could never do that."

Linda, the Depressed Woman

Linda began to engage with the assignments as she had promised, but she remained convinced that they wouldn't help.

The mirror exercise made Linda sad. When I asked her why, she said, "I realized that my life is more than half over and I've never accomplished anything. I'm getting old."

For the music exercise, she listened to Latin American music. "It made me want to dance," she explained with the slightest twinkle in her eye.

I inquired, "Why didn't you?"

She smiled. "I never dance, it's not my thing."

"But it could be?" I suggested.

She looked shy and coquettish at the same time. She then said, "Maybe."

As the days and weeks go by, keep observing the reactions and conditioning of your body, and that of others. Competence in this practice will make you more able to take care of yourself and others.

Chapter 3

History, the Sculptor of Our Being

This show grew out of my idea of Savion Glover [a brilliant African-American tap dancer] as a living repository of rhythm. There are these old black tap dancers who were taught by the old black tap dancers, and so on. All of those guys passed on that information to Savion, and it landed in his feet, and his being, and his soul.
> —GEORGE C. WOLFE, producer of
> *Bring in 'Da Noise; Bring in 'Da Funk*

The mind of which we are unaware is aware of us.
> —R. D. LAING

The first problem for all of us, men and women, is not to learn, but to unlearn.
> —GLORIA STEINEM

From the first two chapters, I hope you have begun to see that your behavior is a reflection of your body's structure, including what we call your mind. But how did your structure become what it is? How were you molded into being who you are and into doing what you do today? One of the privileges of being alive at the beginning of a new millennium is that we have some plausible answers to these central questions of life.

One source of your structure is what you are born with, your *foundational properties*. The abilities to speak, to think, to love, to fight, to build, and to create—these are your gifts from billions of years of evolution. You reap the fruits of countless species that now lie extinct, in the particulars that your parents bestow.

So powerful are these properties that only the most unimaginable circumstances can alter their nature. This was brought home to me when Humberto Maturana told me the tale of the "wolf children." In 1922, two girls, eight and five, were rescued from a remote forest in India. Their parents had abandoned the children. A family of wolves had apparently adopted the girls and raised them in the forest. One child died shortly after being "rescued" by humans. The other lived on for a few more years.

At the time of rescue, the girls walked on all fours, ate only raw meat, and had the nocturnal habits of wolves—they slept during the day and prowled at night. They did not speak. When they were in the company of humans, they were frightened and hid in the corners of rooms. They preferred to spend their time with dogs or wolves.

When they were rescued, their health was excellent. After this, they became depressed and their health deteriorated. The girl who survived developed some human habits such as standing erect, and she learned a few words. But when the moon was full she would go to the window and howl. At times of stress or emotional upset she'd revert to running on all fours and making barking sounds. People who were with her reported that they felt they were with an animal, not a human being.

Linda, the Depressed Woman

Linda was deeply touched by this story of two girls robbed of their full potential. She said, "It's almost as if my parents were wolves. Except they raised me not to hunt, but to think I'm 'stupid.' I've lived 'stupid' like the wolf children lived 'wolf.' I never thought I could do or be anything else.

"In fact, I'm still doing it," she went on. "My future looks like I'll do nothing but barely live."

Human behavior is the result of a weaving of innate and learned experiences. These children had the genetic inheritance of human beings, but they also had the cultural shaping of wolf society. At any moment in time, a triggering event revealed the weaving of these two strands.

How Do the Pulawats Do It?

Now, let's turn to how you learn and how that alters you in the process. Remember in the last chapter I talked about plasticity, the "moldability" of the nervous system, as one of its basic properties. How does this operate in your life? How have you been molded?

Thomas Gladwin, a cultural anthropologist, gives us a vivid story that shows how cultural practices are a major force that shapes us.

Gladwin lived for several years with the Pulawats, a people of the South Pacific who dwell on small and widely scattered islands. The men of this tribe are expert seamen, fishing the prolific tropical waters around their islands. They also often travel hundreds of miles to distant fishing grounds, or to faraway islands for trading.

The Pulawats spend much of their lives in their boats, which are meager fifteen- to twenty-foot sailing canoes with an outrigger pontoon for stability. Gladwin was amazed that these seamen could perform voyages of hundreds of miles in these craft. But what was even more astounding to Gladwin was how the Pulawats navigated when out of sight of land. They had neither maps nor compasses to use for orientation. The Pulawats also had no celestial reckoning instruments to allow the stars to guide them.

So how did the Pulawats sail? Gladwin became determined to learn their navigational secrets. He made friends with several expert seamen and asked them how they steered their ships. The seamen looked at him in puzzlement, as if someone had asked them how they breathed. They replied, "We just do it."

Over time, Gladwin recognized that the seamen had common practices that they had absorbed just by living in their culture and sailing with their fathers, brothers, and others. They then performed these practices without even thinking or "figuring it out." Another way of saying this is that part of being a Pulawat is just having this practice. It's not genetic, but it shows up in all Pulawats, the same way all Japanese bow when greeting one another; they don't think, they just bow.

But what was this navigational practice? In the spirit of a good cultural anthropologist, Gladwin set out to observe the Pulawat sailors. He sailed with them almost daily for months. Along the way he asked lots of questions of the sailors. At first they thought he was crazy. With time, they came to tolerate his inquisitiveness and gave him thoughtful responses. The answer to the mystery emerged.

It seems that the Pulawats live in a part of the South Pacific where there are three kinds of waves, each of which runs in a different direction. The three directions are constant and stable except during great storms. Gladwin discovered that a sailing boat's motion at any instant represents the summation of the forces of the three waves. Since the waves were constant in direction, the rocking of the boat "told" the seamen exactly the direction in which they were headed. What was even more remarkable is that the seamen knew how to get from island to island by picking the right rocking motion!

Midway in his observations, Gladwin went on a short voyage. On the first night he became concerned when the seaman said it was time to sleep. Gladwin's worry grew as the seaman bundled himself up in the bottom of the boat. Gladwin thought, "This is the end. How can he navigate when he's asleep?"

What ensued stunned Gladwin. As the anthropologist huddled in fear at the bow of the boat, the Pulawat seaman would, from time to time, jump up from his slumber, adjust the boat's course, and then go back to sleep. The droning of the seaman's snoring followed. Then, after an interval, the process repeated itself.

Through further questioning, Gladwin learned that the seaman, even in his sleep, sensed that the rocking of the boat had changed, that they were off course. The seaman "knew" of the error even while he was sleeping, much as the mother of a newborn baby can "hear" her child even as the mother sleeps.

Gladwin now understood that the seamen know direction by their relation to the waves. But how did they judge speed? Navigation requires both direction and speed. Again, he was amazed by the explanation that emerged from his observations and questioning. The Pulawats apparently think of a boat as a fixed point. In their minds, their speed is a function of how fast islands and floating objects move past the boat. There are no computers, no calculators to determine this, just the seaman's looking and knowing.

Now Gladwin realized how the Pulawats did it. By reckoning direction and speed, the Pulawats had the two elements necessary to navigate. This system had evolved in their culture because it was effective. If not, there would have been a lot of lost and drowned seamen.

Pulawat youth, Gladwin found, did not learn how to navigate at sailing schools, but by journeying with masters and by doing what the masters did. Soon they were competent to make longer and longer voyages. They apprenticed, practiced, received correction from a master, and eventually were expert navigators, ready to pass on the practice to the next generation of Pulawats.

Robert, the High Achiever

Robert was intrigued by the notion of cultural inheritance. "I came from an Eastern European, Jewish culture," he said. "My family's major priority was social advancement through learning. In my parents' culture, only the learned were valued. A manual profession was never a possibility for me. I never even considered it.

"Since my father was a businessman," he continued, "I had to go the next step. I had to be a professional. It was almost like the culture decided for me. I was to be a doctor or a lawyer. The choice was never mine to make. I am like a Jewish Pulawat."

Later in class, Robert admitted that he resented the fact that it felt like he never made the choice.

From the Pulawats' example you can see that a culture shapes its members in unique ways. What is second nature to a Pulawat is foreign to us. But what relevance does this story hold for people who inhabit the cultures of modern life?

So much of what we call our common sense is culturally determined—driving on the right side of the road, eating fast food, going to the movies on a Friday night, and eating popcorn in the movie theater. Each of these culturally given habits looks like *the* only way to live. But when we travel to new places, we see differently.

In England people drive on the left side. In France, most people abhor fast food. And in Israel, movies are closed on Friday nights because of the Sabbath.

As we go on, remember the "way-it-is" nature of how culture shapes us. We go into the movie, give up our ticket, and automatically move toward or away from the refreshment stand. Can you imagine a movie theater without one? What would be the reaction of the moviegoers? Something would be missing—*really* missing. In France, they have no refreshment stands in movies; eating in public like that is impolite.

Heart Sounds

Cultural common sense is not limited to everyday habits but pervades all realms—everything that we do. In fact, we could say that learning means developing a new common sense.

One of the symbols of the medical culture, something that every physician knows about and can use, is a stethoscope. In his or her first year of schooling, every medical student learns to listen to a heart and from the sounds to make assessments of its physiology and state of function.

One day before my initial coached session in examining hearts, I walked through a torrential rainstorm to Sparr's drugstore to get my first stethoscope. I was filled with excitement and pride—the stethoscope symbolized the reality of my dream of becoming a doctor. Sparr's drugstore, then as now, sits on a corner near the Harvard Medical School. Unchanged for decades, Sparr's features an old-fashioned soda fountain, cramped aisles bulging with cakes, candies, walkers, and canes, and glass cases jammed with every possible instrument needed by medical students.

"Which one is the best stethoscope?" I asked Joe Sparr, pharmacist and owner of the establishment. "It depends on who's listening," he answered. This confused me. Sensing a lost sale, Joe probably decided not to be philosophical and pointed to a glass case and said, "This is the one Sam Levine uses." (Dr. Levine was a venerable and well-known cardiologist at the Harvard-affiliated Peter Bent Brigham Hospital.) "I'll take that one then," I replied with the fervor of someone hoping to play as well as Itzhak Perlman because he buys a Stradivarius.

That night in my dorm I poured over the guide to listening to a heart. I memorized facts about heart sounds, murmurs, split sounds, normal and abnormal rhythms. By midnight I was well prepared for the next day's class. I was especially confident with my "Levine" stethoscope.

The next morning, Dr. McNeely, my physical diagnosis instructor, led me and my fellow students to the bedside of a patient who had been warned that we were novices. Dr. McNeely introduced us and then left to visit with his own patients. I was first up. My cockiness about hearing hearts dissolved as soon as I placed my stethoscope on the patient's chest. What I heard resembled the clang and clatter of a subway terminal. None of the textbook's clearly described sounds, murmurs, and rhythms was present. All I heard was a cacophony. The patient, who must have sensed my panic, whispered, "I have a systolic murmur."

After an hour of various attempts by us to hear the patient's heart problem, Dr. McNeely rejoined the class. He laughed in knowing amusement as I told him that I didn't know what I had heard, but that the patient had given me the answer.

"Come with me, Matt," he said. Dr. McNeely put his stethoscope next to mine on the patient's chest and said, "I'll tap your hand each time I hear the first heart sound." He did this, and gradually I began to hear it. "Now for the second heart sound," he added, and repeated the procedure. And so on, even including the murmur. I had it now. Or so I thought.

We met again the next week and I was assigned another patient. I was dismayed to find that the same thing happened all over again. I couldn't tell one heart sound from another. McNeely patiently repeated his routine.

Each ensuing week I began to hear more as I visited each patient. The sounds were different one from the other, the murmur was clearly different from the sounds, and I could describe the murmur. By the end of the course, if I listened carefully and for a long time to each heart that I examined, I could come pretty close to the professor's description.

I noticed another thing. With each session, I heard and diagnosed the sounds in less time. In the first examination, even after an hour, I couldn't tell one sound from another. Later, it took just a few minutes of concentrated effort and I had the answer.

Now I'm going to tell you a secret that I never reveal to my patients. After years of practice, I don't even think about listening to a heart when I examine one. I just listen, like the Pulawat just sails. In fact, sometimes when I'm examining a heart, I'm thinking of something else—What's wrong with this person? What diagnosis could this be? I have embodied the heart examination; it's in my structure.

However, if an abnormality exists I come to full alert, identify the abnormality, and make diagnostic assessments, just like the Pulawat sailor does when he senses a shift in the waves. But during the flow of a normal examination I'm on automatic; my body is functioning like a machine.

By this point, you can understand when I make this somewhat unusual statement: A doctor is a person who has entered into practices typical of the culture of medicine so that his or her structure has been modified to perform the practices of a doctor. And the practices I've learned are the ones that my medical culture has shown me.

There are other traditions that a physician embodies: the Hippocratic tradition of respect for the patient, the Samaritan tradition of caring and compassion. For the most part, these traditions are transmitted and embodied by immersion, not by instruction.

Culture Shapes Our Common Sense

The era that you live in, your family, your culture, your work or profession, the unique experiences you have, both joyful and traumatic, all mold your structure as you embody them.

For example, Shimon Peres, the former Israeli prime minister, acknowledged in a *New Yorker* article the profound impact that the culture and history of the Middle East have on the people of the region. After his electoral defeat, Peres received thousands of letters. One was from a seventeen-year-old boy, an invalid from birth who was confined to a wheelchair. Peres confided, "He wrote me something which I thought was very deep. He said, 'There is something we can learn from our private lives for our national life. Everybody may think that if I would be asked what is the most important thing I would like to have in my life, naturally it is to get rid of invalidism and serve in the Army. But it is not a simple proposition. *I am at the same time afraid of becoming normal and facing daily life.*' " (Italics mine.)

Peres said that the same thing happens to nations: "Because of wars, we become invalids, we are afraid to try something else, more normal." The decades of conflict in the Middle East have profoundly altered the structure of many Israelis and of the nation itself. It has become suspicious, fixed in attitude, and fearful.

I saw an example of Peres's insights a few years ago in a class I was teaching. One of my patients, William, was a thirty-three-year-old African-American firefighter. Bright and ambitious, William loved his job. He was slated for promotion to fire chief at his local station.

Unfortunately, William lived and worked in a blue-collar, racially segregated town. His fellow firefighters and his superior officers often said or did things that enraged him. During many of these episodes he had begun to have the chest pains associated with moments of anger. His physician feared that if this went on, William would develop heart disease.

In the course of working with William, I asked him, "Why do fools make you so angry?" He looked at me in amazement for asking the question. I then said, "Who pays the price for your anger? Do you know that black people have a higher incidence of heart disease than white people? They may be fools for speaking and believing as they do; what about you for reacting as you react? You are as automatic as they are!"

"Damn it, man, we have a lot to be angry about!" William replied in righteous indignation. "Are you a racist, too?"

"Maybe so," I answered. "But isn't attaining your goal of being fire chief more important to you than being right and angry? If you die of heart disease, you're only going to please the bigots."

William grew quiet and reflective. After the class he approached me and thanked me for being so direct with him. I asked him another question: "Why are you so quick to anger over any negative statement?"

William thought for a moment and said, "I guess that's just the way I am."

I suggested to William that he embodied a historic habit common among people who have suffered persecution and discrimination. With each phrase that I spoke, I could see William's body reacting in anger. I would stop, have him observe where his body had taken him, and return to our conversation. I added, "William, what you need to consider is the possibility of freeing yourself from your culturally given, consuming anger. Would you rather be right, or healthy?"

William worked hard at the course's distinctions. With diligence, he began to observe his automatic, cultural reaction of anger. When he did this, sometimes it abated under his very gaze.

Fast forward two years. William is now chief of his local fire department.

Gretchen, the Perfectionist

Gretchen recalled the impact of her family's culture on her life. She said, "In my house, there were only two possibilities: right or wrong, good or evil. My religious teaching was very strict. My life was lived between extremes—I was either perfect or I was worthless. My fear is that I'll make a mess of things. It's as if left to my own devices I'll always be wrong and bad. It's scary."

Like the Pulawat navigator, she said, "I awaken from sleep thinking that I'm off course. I'm always off course, but I'm not sure where the true course is. I've learned to expect it to come from an outside instruction from my mother."

Your habits of action, your thinking and perception, your competencies as well as your limitations are greatly shaped by the culture that surrounds you.

As you embody your history you become a new person, a unique person. When you're triggered, you act in a unique way, like Barbara did with her asthma attack. Gerald Edelman entitled one of his books *The Remembered Present,* a wonderfully poignant phrase that describes how your history is manifested in the present moment.

As you read these lines, I encourage you to reflect upon how your history, your personal Remembered Present, has shaped you. You'll enter into this exploration in a deeper way in the exercises, but for now think how your cultural background, your family, your schooling, your work experiences, your romantic experiences have shaped your life.

Emotional Learning

Thus far I've talked about how history shapes you in terms of skills and cultural and personal habits. Historic learning also occurs at the level of emotions.

Joseph LeDoux has written an informative book about emotional learning called *The Emotional Brain.* In it, he describes the anatomical and physiological aspects of how our structures become shaped and molded to exhibit certain emotional responses. I'll describe one aspect of this phenomenon—post-traumatic stress disorder (PTSD)—and leave for chapter 5 a further discussion of emotional learning.

Before describing PTSD, you have to learn a little neuroanatomy— the anatomy of the brain. The brain contains a structure called the *amygdala* (from the Greek word for "almond"), which is present in humans, but also in many other animal species. This region of the brain receives sensory stimuli—signals from the outside world. When the amygdala is activated, it produces an alarm response, which assists the animal in avoiding or fleeing from threat. This response is expressed through stress hormones, adrenal hormones, and mobilization of the muscles of movement and of the heart. The hormones produce in an instant widespread changes in the body's chemistry.

At times, the alarm response is essential for keeping a person or animal safe. For example, this response may be appropriate when you're facing an oncoming speeding automobile while crossing the street. But for some people, this response occurs without an apparent external threat. (More about this later on.)

With experience, the amygdala's response is susceptible to learning—i.e., structural change. For instance, the trigger that activates this mechanism can become significantly more sensitive, so that it "fires off" with less stimulus. This change in threshold involves chemical or structural changes in the nervous system itself. For our purposes, this mechanism can "learn," and the learning is *emotional learning.*

PTSD illustrates one kind of emotional learning. People suffering from PTSD have experienced a traumatic situation far outside the realm of normal life, such as the horrors of war, parental abuse, rape, etc. During such an event, the body's danger signals bombard the amygdala. This heightens its activity and makes it extremely sensitive to subsequent signals. Other sights, sounds, and smells associated with the event—the clap of a gunshot, the flash of an explosion, or the cry of a person in pain—somehow become linked in the brain with the traumatic event and its mobilizing response.

At a later moment, an event like one of the associated stimuli, such as the slamming of a screen door or the flash of a firecracker, triggers the body's massive conditioned response. To make matters worse, the conscious part of the brain (most of what I have described up to this point happens unconsciously) then experiences the array of body changes of the automatic mobilization—the stress response. This gives rise to anxiety, worry, and explicit memories of old events. These additional thoughts may further arouse the amygdala and heighten anxiety. A vicious circle is established, and the result can be debilitating.

Walter, the Angry Man

Walter was intrigued by the discussion of automatic fear reactions. "I'm not afraid of very much," he said angrily. I asked him why he was angry. He responded, "Who's angry? I'm not." His tone and volume triggered in me a fear reaction—"Get out quick!" My amygdala response kicked in.

"Maybe it's just me," I said, "but you sound angry to me." I asked the class: "Is this true for anyone else?" Every hand shot up.

One woman in the class admitted that she wanted to cry out in fear every time Walter spoke. "He's scary," she said.

At first, Walter grew even more furious because of his classmates' assessment. But then he settled back in his chair, looking thoughtful. It was the first time that I had ever seen him in this mood.

Drifting

Experience molds the nervous system and the whole body so that their responses to future events or thoughts are altered. I have examined this on many levels of human behavior, from the emotions to sailing a boat. It's a universal truth.

In this chapter, I set out to examine how your structure became what it is so that you respond as you do to life's events. A large part is what you inherited from your ancestry, what you were given historically. On the foundation of your inheritance, who you are today is the result of the molding experiences of the "drift" of living your particular life.

Understanding your history does not change who you are, but it gives you a sense of coherence. You can see yourself as an unfolding organism, as a work in progress. As long as you are alive, you can alter your structure with new practices, with new learning.

The wolf children's unique "drift" rendered them somewhere between human and wolf. When returned from the forest, one was able to learn some human habits; the other was so uncoupled from her "natural" environment that she could not exist and died. The Pulawats' "drift" showed how culture can convey unique skill and competence by putting people into effective practices. In this way, their nervous system is changed to support a new repertoire of activities. This was true of my learning how to listen to a patient's heartbeat.

Finally I suggested that, in addition to your thoughts, actions, and identities, how you feel emotionally is partly learned. LeDoux's work shows that much of your emotional life and your mood lives in the structural characteristics of your nervous system. In chapter 5, I'll go deeper into the area of emotional learning, but for now I want you to engage in a little reflection.

Begin to reflect on how your historic drift has shaped some of your basic beliefs about money, family, career, racial difference, men, women, etc. Start to observe some of your automatic thoughts, opinions, emotions, preferences, and fears. Also begin to reflect on how you learned these reactions.

As you do, I want you to realize that this may provoke some uncomfortable feelings. When some people begin to grasp their automaticity—the degree to which much of their life is lived as machinelike response to the environment—they fall into a mood of hopelessness and despair. It's as if they say to themselves, "Oh my God, I'm like a machine, I have so many bad habits. I'll never be happy." If you're feeling this, read Linda's reactions.

Linda, the Depressed Woman

Linda admitted that she had fallen into a mood of hopelessness and despair.

In fact, Linda told me after one class that "I took this course to get better, and now I feel worse. If I'm a stupidity machine, what hope is there for me?"

I said that I understood how it looked to her. I told her that what she was going through was a crucial part of the learning process. I invited her (and you the reader) to be patient. Then I asked her the following question: "Do you see how expertly and skillfully you have lived out the 'stupid' narrative in your life? What if it's not the truth, just a story, and you're really an excellent learner? The problem is that you have learned a very destructive story." Linda began to cry.

I have compassion for but do not agree with Linda's sense of despair. I know that for all of us learning can continue throughout life, and that habits that at one time looked critical for survival but are now destructive can, at least to some degree, be changed.

Learning occurs most powerfully when you acknowledge fully what you are at this very moment with truthfulness and authenticity, and also compassion. You are your history, in this special sense. If you accept this, then you'll be able to learn and improve your relationships, your self-expression, and your well-being. If you reject this, you'll spend the rest of your life looking for an imaginary "right" world of safety.

EXERCISES

Major Points in Chapter 3

☐ You are born with a genetic inheritance, the raw material of your being. This establishes a *foundation of possibility* for you.

☐ In addition to what you share with all humans, you are unique because of your own biological structure, which has been shaped by your life experiences. This shaping occurs in your cells and organs as you learn, and especially in your brain. The brain is the most plastic of your organs.

☐ Culture, family, and social class also shape you without your awareness. The Pulawat story shows this—Pulawat sailors learn their style of navigation just by growing up in their culture.

☐ In addition, you also learn by intention, as you did when you enrolled in driving school or took ice skating lessons. At first, you needed a teacher to provide you with clear distinctions for action. With practice and repetition your body changed and you could drive a car or skate without even thinking. Driving and skating now live in your body—you *are* a driver or skater.

☐ History shapes your body in all these ways. When you act, or when you react (your remembered present), your history speaks *through* your body.

☐ In this way, your history "shows" you a world and how to act and live in it. But at the same time, it limits your freedom, your possibilities. The Arab-Israeli conflict, as described by Shimon Peres, shows how the combatants' thinking is so filled with blame and fear that peace will never occur without reshaping not just *what* the combatants think, but *how* they think. This is what leaders and great teachers do—they show the historic nature of our positions and invite us to build new possibilities for being and living.

☐ History shapes not only your cognitive life (what you know) but your emotional life (the state of your body). You react to a test, to learning, to challenge, to loss, to life itself in a stereotyped, learned way.

☐ Awareness of your historically shaped reactions is the first step toward finding freedom's door.

A Brief Check on Previous Learning

In exercises for chapter 1, you began to examine yourself as a learner. How are you doing with your meditation practice? Are you able to find time to meditate each day?

Do you still find yourself expecting some instantaneous and tangible result from this practice? It's a subtle practice and yields its gifts with time. Be patient and notice if it's hard for you to be patient.

Are you still plagued by "Am I doing it right?" questions? My instructor taught me to meditate by saying, "Sit down and be quiet." It's that simple!

Begin to notice thoughts that come automatically as you meditate. Thoughts of things to do, tasks, regrets, fears, etc. Also notice feelings and emotions that come up for you as you meditate. Can you begin to put a name on different emotions and moods?

Become aware of sensations of all kinds in your body: in your bladder, in your back and neck, in your chest, in your eyes. Just keep noticing. The awareness muscle is built by practice.

In chapter 2's exercise section, we examined the state of your body in a variety of situations. Are you beginning to become more competent in observing yourself and others? Have you begun to see that your body is always changing? One moment your muscles are relaxed or not even in your awareness; the next moment your neck is tight, you are off center.

Keep building your skill for observing your body.

Exercises for Reflection and Learning

The exercises in this chapter help increase your awareness of how history has shaped you to react as you do today, to see the world that you see, and to do what you do.

These exercises also help you observe that your body is wherever you are. This may sound obvious, but you may be blind to what your body is telling you about you. Your body doesn't know *the* truth, but it does know *your* truth.

At the same time, what is true for you may not be what is true for me. Learning how to live in relationship with other people involves allowing both your view and those of others to be valid. We call this "re-spect"—

seeing the world again through the eyes of another. Building body awareness helps you to take care of yourself and respect others.

Such awareness benefits you in two ways. First, you realize that the way you are today is a natural expression of what you've learned. You see a coherence in your life that allows you to be at peace with what exists at this moment. The past is past. What was, was. You learned what you had to learn and survived. Second, if you can see that you learned to be the way that you are, then you can acknowledge that you're a good learner. What you learned earlier may no longer be useful. But because you're such a good learner, you have a tremendous capacity to learn new practices and to build a different body for your current needs and ambitions.

History—Exercise One: the Photo Exercise

This exercise involves finding photos from different stages of your life—at infancy, childhood, adolescence, and young adulthood. Also use recent pictures of yourself like passport photos, licenses, picture IDs, family photos. Wedding or confirmation photos are also acceptable.

Examine each photo. Then, in the notes section below, describe yourself at that age. Use words such as *happy, confident, smart, rebellious, in love, frightened,* etc. Let your memory take you back to the time of the photo.

Next write down a memory of an important event that happened at that time of your life. Remember that event in as much detail as possible. What happened? How did you feel? Who was present? What did you do? What emotions were present?

When I did this exercise, I was struck by a picture of myself when I was at Amherst College. I seemed to be so young and perfect—I was wearing stylish clothes, I had a slick haircut, my body was lean and muscular. I remembered how well I was doing in school at the time. But the picture also triggered memories of how hard I had to work to achieve such academic excellence. A great deal of anxiety accompanied this pursuit of high marks. I felt then, and would for many years thereafter, that whatever I did wasn't good enough. This behavior and those emotions are still in my body, but now I can see them and focus more on what I *want* to do, rather than on what I *have* to do to meet the expectations of others.

Childhood Photograph

Age:

What was important to me at that time?

An important event was . . .

What did I do?

How did it feel?

Do I see this behavior in me now?

Adolescent Photograph

Age:

What was important to me at that time?

An important event was . . .

What did I do?

How did it feel?

Do I see this behavior in me now?

Early Adulthood Photograph

Age:

What was important to me at that time?

An important event was . . .

What did I do?

How did it feel?

Do I see this behavior in me now?

Midlife Photograph

Age:

What was important to me at that time?

An important event was . . .

What did I do?

How did it feel?

Do I see this behavior in me now?

Current Photograph

Age:

What is important to me now?

An important event happening is . . .

What am I doing?

How does it feel?

Is this an old behavior? From when?

Notes
(History—Exercise One)

History—Exercise Two: Writing the Story of Another Person

Here, I want you to pretend you're a great fiction writer like Ernest Hemingway, Toni Morrison, or John Updike by writing the story of another person. This exercise helps you see that who you are at this moment is the manifestation, in your body and in your self, of the historic sweep of your life. There is no right or wrong about how you are. It's just the way you are. You may want to change, to learn, but you can only do this from the ground on which you stand.

Choose someone to write about who you know casually—an acquaintance, not a close friend, associate, or family member. This forces you to use more of your imagination.

Close your eyes and picture this person as you know him or her. What are his/her characteristic moods? Does he/she have self-respect and dignity? Is he/she optimistic or pessimistic about the future? What are her/his social and speech patterns? Is he/she defensive or a learner? How does he/she carry his/her body? Is he/she confident or self-doubting? Make these and other assessments of the person you're thinking about.

After you have a clear picture of this person in your thoughts, write a one-page fictional biography of this person's life in the space below. What was his/her infancy and childhood like? What was his/her family like? What are his/her religious and social traditions? What major successes and defeats has this person had? How is his/her social life? What other parts of his/her history have shaped how he/she is today?

Fictional Biography

.

Did you see that certain stories or events "fit" with your fictional character and some don't? We all have that coherence. The source of this coherence is our body, which moves through history, recording the past and generating the future.

History—Exercise Three: Your History

Now it's your turn to hold the mirror on yourself. This exercise works best if you do it all at one sitting.

1. Review your notes on the previous exercises in this section.
2. Now, in the pages that I've provided below, write your own auto-biography. You may want to use chronological order, or to build it around themes. Write a narrative about who you are today as a result of the life that you have lived so far. Write about your family, about teachers, about major events that have shaped your life. Write about your memories, your successes, and your failures.
3. In your autobiography include:

   □ Your pervasive moods
   □ How you are as a learner
   □ Your body reactions and state
   □ Your career choices
   □ Your social life with friends
   □ Your intimate social life
   □ Your attitudes toward sex, money, and power

My Autobiography

My Autobiography

Now that you have finished, take a moment to stretch and unwind. Use deep breathing to bring your body into the present in a relaxed way. Now read your autobiography, and as you do, ask yourself:

- ☐ What is your mood as you read it?
- ☐ What do you see about how the pieces of your life fit together?
- ☐ What do you see about the major turning points in your life?
- ☐ What do you see about yourself as a learner?

Before leaving these exercises, see if you can look at your history with acceptance, forgiveness, and compassion. Accept yourself in this moment and recommit, if you choose, to change and learning. You can forgive yourself fully. Let blame, resentment, remorse go. They are not useful.

In these exercises you've been exploring the biological connection between your past and the present. Your history has shaped your body to behave the way it does today—to see, do, feel, and act as you do. Your systems are working well. You are a great learner.

The Experiences of My Patients in Doing These Exercises

Gretchen, the Perfectionist

These exercises showed Gretchen that her life was driven by a pervasive family teaching—always do the right thing, always follow the rules. In her family, play for its own sake, joy, and laughter were not accepted or admired.

When something new challenged her, or she didn't know the rules of a particular situation, Gretchen became upset and anxious, as if danger lurked around the next bend of the road.

As she looked at her pictures, Gretchen saw a playful infant who by the age of five had become vigilant and hypersensitive to the approval of others.

Walter, the Angry Man

Walter recalled that violence had been pervasive in his life from the very beginning. His father reacted to disappointment by beating

Walter, his brothers, and his mother. His father's rage was terrifying, especially when he was drinking.

Walter saw that he learned this pattern of dealing with disappointment. When he was displeased, rage overtook him. Walter also began to understand that he was very distrustful. While looking at a picture of himself in his grammar school basketball uniform, Walter remembered the day that his father promised to come to his game but didn't show up. He was in a bar drinking. Walter realized that this incident, along with many others in his childhood, "taught" him that he should not trust people because they would break their promises. This distrust and his violent habits were his childhood inheritance.

Robert, the High Achiever

Robert's early pictures showed a serious child who rarely smiled. As Robert looked at these pictures, he could hear voices from his past saying, "What a smart child Robert is." His family never called him Bob—that name was too pedestrian for such a bright child.

Robert recalled that each grade he received in school was directly connected to future success by his parents' comments: "Do well in junior high school so you can get into the advanced class in high school; do well in the advanced class so you can get into Harvard; do well so you can be a doctor or a lawyer." He remembered wanting a career in law before he even knew what a lawyer was.

Robert never experienced inner satisfaction, the joy of having done well. The theme was "What is my next challenge on the path to success" without his ever really knowing what a successful life was.

Linda, the Depressed Woman

As she did these exercises, Linda shifted from a mood of resignation to one of curiosity. When she heard me say, "You're really an excellent learner, you learned the lessons of the past well," she saw the irony of the statement as well as the ability it described.

The exercises showed that in Linda's mind her father and

mother preferred her brothers to her. They often called Linda "stupid" and told her a career was out of the question. Linda came to believe this deeply.

Linda's husband was much like her father. He had even said in public, "You can't expect much from Linda." This hurt her, but she also feared that it was the truth.

Chapter 4

You Are What You Say

Basic words do not state something that might exist outside
them; by being spoken they establish a mode of existence.
 —MARTIN BUBER

You must give birth to your images. They are the future waiting to be born.
 —RAINER MARIA RILKE

The thought manifests as the word;
The word manifests as the deed;
The deed develops into habit;
And the habit hardens into character;
So watch the thought and its ways with care;
And let it spring from love
Born out of concern for all beings.

As the shadow follows the body,
As we think, so we become.
 —From the *Dhammapada* (the sayings of the Buddha)

This chapter is about language, perhaps our most uniquely
human characteristic.

Language is difficult to discuss. We can look at an orange and describe it in words—it is almost round, it has a crinkled skin, it has a fra-
grance, it is orange-colored, etc. Not much confusion here. But when it
comes to describing language, it becomes more complicated because
language can only be described with words—that is, in language itself. In

this chapter I will *show* rather than *describe* language, and the various actions that people take in language. Some of you may think it strange that I speak of "actions in language," but I'll explain this shortly.

In Language You Generate Life

Fernando Flores is a Chilean of great intellect and a wide range of expertise, including Western philosophy, computer science, business and organizational behavior, and entrepreneurship. A bear of a man—six feet, 250 pounds—he's a great synthesizer and weaver of threads from different traditions. I suspect that someday he'll be seen as one of this generation's great thinkers.

But Fernando is more than an intellectual—he's a man of enormous courage. In 1973, Salvador Allende, Chile's democratically elected president, died in a bloody coup. Fernando was then the country's minister of finance. As a result of his activities, he was imprisoned, subjected to mock trials, and punished with solitary confinement. For three years Fernando was separated from his wife and five children. Fernando's case attracted the attention of Amnesty International, which helped to negotiate his release from prison in 1976. He then came to the United States and completed a Ph.D. program at the University of California at Berkeley. He is now a world-famous business consultant who uses his insights into language to transform companies and people.

Being in prison changed Fernando's life. He emerged from jail with a new vision, a new understanding, and a new commitment to the fundamental connections between language and actions. As he says, "I never told a victim story about my imprisonment. Instead, I told a transformation story—about how prison changed my outlook, about how I saw that communication, truth, and trust are at the heart of power. I made my own assessment of my life, and I began to live it. That was freedom."

Fernando speaks these words in broken English (he calls it "Spanglish"), which makes it difficult to understand him. But what makes his words even more difficult to comprehend is the philosophical picture of the world that he paints. It's not that what he's saying is complicated. In fact, it's quite simple. Yet it's so contrary to our common sense that when people first hear his ideas, they make "no sense" at the reasoning level.

As I said in chapter 2, I met Fernando at the same seminar where I encountered Humberto Maturana's revolutionary views on biology. As Maturana finished his discourse, he set the stage for Fernando to describe language as a unique feature of human life. It was a Chilean one-two punch of mammoth proportions for me, my work, and for the lives of others who have embodied what they were saying.

Fernando began his lecture with this statement: "In language we build our own identities, our relationships with others, the countries that we live in, the companies we have, and the values that we hold dear. With language we generate life. Without language we are mostly chimpanzees."

"This is preposterous!" I said to myself. "How can he be so sure?" I even asked him that question. He refused to answer me directly but said, "Let me show you. Let me show everybody here at the seminar" (some one hundred people). To do this, Fernando asked us to repeat in unison and with a deep, loud, whole-body voice what he was about to say (I suggest that you read the next lines in the same manner):

Life seems hopeless, bleak even. I have nowhere to turn. No one to turn to. What is more ominous still is that this will never change.

After we finished, Fernando reminded us to say the next statement in the same manner as we had the last one. Then he began again:

Nothing will help. There is no one to turn to. It feels like the Almighty has forgotten me. Times are hard. They will not get better. They will probably get even worse, though this is beyond imagination.

As the last words reverberated throughout the hall, I felt a heaviness in my chest that weighed about a ton. The problems in my life appeared before me—my inability to help my patients, the unhappiness I felt over my recent divorce, the sense of loneliness that pervaded my private life. Other people reacted in a different way. Several sobbed, a number laughed nervously. Most sat stunned in amazement at what was happening. Fernando as if by magic had changed the mood of each individual in the room.

I asked myself, "How did this happen? How did saying these words shift the way my body felt?" Just then Fernando asked, "What actions are you likely to take or not take in the mood that you are now in?"

I remember thinking to myself that in this mood antidepressants looked like a good option. Ambition or creativity seemed impossible.

The person next to me remarked, "In this mood, all I feel like doing is crawling into a hole."

"Do you see?" Fernando bellowed from behind the podium. "Do you see that your speaking has changed your body, your mood, your physiology, and your possibilities for action? Language has generated a moment of life for you. The action of languaging changed you like a drug. Even though you rationally knew that this was only an exercise, it happened anyway."

As I sat there at the Cronkhite Center, I added Fernando's teachings to those of Maturana's as "must learns." Humberto's vision had shown me the importance of biology in understanding life, knowing, and learning. Fernando's brilliance on that day, and in the years ahead, would help me become clearer and clearer about the centrality of language to human life.

Discovering Language

The story of Helen Keller helps show the core nature of language for human living. For most of us, Helen's life serves as an example of courage in facing adversity and not letting physical limitations ruin your life. As you probably know, Helen was born a normal child, but early in her infancy she was stricken with meningitis, an infectious disease that left her deaf and blind. Yet she eventually graduated from Radcliffe and helped build several institutions for the education of the blind.

For me, however, the most amazing moment in her life was when she discovered language. As a child, Helen was uncontrollable and unruly. She was almost like an animal in her reactions—affectionate and clinging, and given to violent tantrums—somewhat like the wolf children in an earlier chapter. To help her, Helen's parents brought in a teacher of the deaf named Anne Sullivan.

One day when Helen was about five, Sullivan decided to introduce words to her. Of course, Sullivan could use neither spoken words nor written symbols to accomplish her goal. Instead, she devised an imaginative approach to the problem. Helen tells the story in her autobiography:

> We walked to the well-house. Someone was drawing water and my teacher placed my hand under the spout. As the cool stream gushed over one hand, she spelled into the other hand the word *water* first slowly, then rapidly.

I was at first annoyed, I did not know what she was doing. As she persisted I stood still, my whole attention fixed upon the motions of her fingers. Suddenly, I felt a misty consciousness as if of something forgotten, a thrill of returning thought; and somehow the mystery of language was revealed to me. I knew then that w-a-t-e-r that Anne was writing into my hand meant that wonderful cool something that was flowing over my hand. That living word awakened my soul, gave it light, hope and joy, set it free!

I have read and told this story dozens of times, and each time I do it moves me. It is the gift of a brilliant, courageous woman reflecting on that moment in life when language was made available to her. Helen could now see how the action of language (using language is an action) opened up a universe of life to her that previously remained hidden.

For Helen and for all of us, language makes possible coordinating with others to create contracts, communities for learning and living, new processes and procedures. It also allows people to become aware of themselves and others and builds trust, intimacy, and, yes, suffering. We can't even imagine life without language. If you try, notice that you are imagining in language itself.

If language is so central to human life in all of its dimensions, then part of our attempt to create a new awareness of mind and body must involve building linguistic awareness, facility, and competence. You are in language already all of the time. But you are not skillful at observing it because you have no powerful distinctions for doing so. With skill at observation comes more success in life and less suffering. This will become clearer as we go on.

In the remainder of this chapter, I'll show how habitual and unconscious incompetence with language can cause suffering in your life. Then I will provide you with a number of distinctions that will allow you to watch how your use of language shapes your life. In the exercise section for this chapter, you will have the opportunity to practice language skills, which has the potential to greatly alter how you think, interact, and feel.

Be patient as you read this chapter. I found that when I began to study how language generates life, it literally made me dizzy at times, along with making me uncomfortable and confused. I forced myself to stay with it. So must you. In time I began to see results and the possibility for valuable change. You will too. In the end, you will live with a new and powerful set of distinctions. Remember, distinctions help us to live more powerfully with what is already happening.

Do Dogs Suffer?

Otto is our family dog. He is a beautiful yellow Lab, a faithful pet, a loving member of our family. He is also a good learner. But Otto is not human; he doesn't "live in a house of language," as the philosopher Martin Heidegger said that humans do. A story about Otto will illustrate life with and without the human capacity for language.

One cold Saturday last winter, my wife, Roz, myself, and Otto arrived midmorning at our Maine house to spend the weekend. As Otto romped through the snowy woods, I built a fire inside and turned on the furnace. It was a typical Maine day in January when the air is so cold that it almost feels solid as it attacks your skin. As we waited for the house to warm up, Roz and I unloaded the car and unpacked our suitcases. After thirty minutes or so, the house was finally comfortable. I called Otto in from his wintry romp to sit with us by the fire.

As Otto entered the house, Roz and I noticed that he was favoring one of his paws. When he positioned one of his legs in a certain way he gave a small yelp, as if in pain. Nonetheless, Otto settled down by the fire and soon was snoozing. He was content, but not Roz, who loves Otto dearly. She began to worry. "What do you think he did to himself?" she asked. "Maybe he broke a bone somehow and we should take him to a veterinarian." As Roz continued her speculations, her brow lined with concern. "I've heard that Labs are prone to hip dysplasia and prostate cancer. Could this be a first sign of a bad disease?"

Roz, being a human, has the capacity to worry. What is worry, really? It's your ability to build a picture in language of "what could be" in the future—a picture that looks frightening or dangerous—and then fall into a mood that corresponds to that picture as if it were "true." What you forget is that you are the artist drawing the picture. Once you imagine this world, your body does the rest. It does what your historical structure allows you to do when you worry. Some people jump into action. Some become paralyzed and anxious. Others deny the concern. Some individuals distract their worries using food, alcohol, music, or TV.

As Roz painted a picture of a world with a sick Otto in it, she automatically triggered emotions of anxiety and nervousness. They were her reactions to the world that she herself had constructed.

Meanwhile, Otto still lay by the fire, fast asleep. Otto wasn't worried, he didn't have language. Roz, on the other hand, was now so worried about Otto that her forehead and neck muscles tightened. Soon she asked me for a neck massage to ease the pain that had developed in her body. Even though the frightening future that concerned Roz existed only in her thoughts, the pain in her neck and forehead were *real*. Her body and her story were in exact alignment.

After a few more minutes of worrying, we walked into the kitchen to get some food, always a way in our family of dealing with personal concerns. As we did, Otto sprang up and followed us in anticipation of getting his daily "doggie cookie." Apparently the injury he had sustained in the woods had eased, or the pulled muscle had relaxed, and he now was walking without a trace of a limp. Roz's neck pain, however, lasted for several hours.

This story illustrates one aspect of the profound difference between a life with and without language. Pain happens to the body; suffering is a function of language. I see this distinction continually in my practice. A patient of mine, Conrad, who is seventy-six, has various aches and pains, the kind that all people experience with aging. Conrad's physical problems have a minimal impact on his life. But his worrying about what they imply is with him twenty-four hours a day and has left him an emotional cripple. "What does this mean?" he asks himself over and again whenever he feels a pain. Other questions race through Conrad's mind: "What could it be? Will it get worse? When will it get better? Could it be cancer?" He has small pains and big suffering.

I hope these examples help you to understand a little better the difference between life with and without language, and how language can lead to suffering. Now, let's discover what language is and how being able to observe your use of it in a powerful way can make you more effective and reduce your suffering.

Communication About Coordination

My friend Bill is in the middle of an acrimonious divorce. Since he was served with divorce papers seven months ago, Bill's continual preoccupation has been to blame his estranged wife, Martha, for a variety of issues, such as spending too much money, neglecting his needs, talking with their mutual friends, and ruining their marriage. This narrative renders Bill angry, powerless, and depressed. He walks around with a continually furrowed forehead, is short-tempered, and is sleeping poorly.

Martha is not going to change no matter how much Bill blames her. In fact, his blaming just makes Martha more defensive and forces her to take precautionary legal moves, such as auditing their joint checking account.

Seven months of a narrative of blame is also making Bill ill. He has chronic fatigue as a result of not sleeping and has lost a great deal of weight. His friends have supported and encouraged him, but he continues to blame and suffer. He never asks himself, "What actions must I take and with whom so that I feel less of a victim?"

Every time that I point out to Bill that his victim-ridden blaming is making him miserable, he retorts that it's all Martha's fault. He has no sense that his life is being shaped by his language. He's the victim of his own narrative and can't see his role in the generation of his own imprisonment. Most importantly, I can't get Bill to understand what language is—*communication about coordination*—just by telling him to stop. He hears this like an accusation. He must learn something. Bill's lack of awareness of the very nature of language deprives him of a powerful focus for observation and action. Of course he uses language; he speaks all the time. We all do. But in his blindness about what language really is, he's actually more "blind" than Helen Keller, and he suffers in his blindness.

So for Bill's sake and for all of us, let's begin to look at what language really is. Human beings coordinate behavior at the action level like all animals. Think of the beautiful coordination between a pair of Olympic pairs skaters. Certainly they have to discuss, rehearse, learn, and practice their routines. But the real beauty and grace happens in the performance itself. It's at the same level of coordination as a flock of geese, or a school of fish; their behavior happens without language, out of their biological capacities. Action flows before or without thought, almost instinctively.

The area of human somatic coupling is not very well recognized, or well understood. But it operates anyhow. Some people make us uneasy just by their presence. Others, like Robin Williams, make us laugh. We are affected by the bodies of others.

But at the human level we not only coordinate behavior at the somatic or physical level, we also coordinate our coordination of behavior in language. What a mouthful! But stay with me and you'll see something wonderful about our unique gift and learn to be more observant and effective with it. If language is the foundation upon which human life is

built, on which we construct our human interactions and even our notion of self, then competence in language will bring you more satisfaction, joy, and effectiveness in living. This is my claim. This is why we're
having this discussion—it has very practical consequences. My work
with thousands of patients bears this out; the work of Dr. Flores in
dozens of organizations bears this out. When people become aware of
their behavior in the linguistic domain, they achieve greater effectiveness, greater satisfaction, and a better mood.

Let's begin with a quote from Humberto Maturana himself about the
phenomenon of language:

> Suppose that every morning my cat meows and runs to the refrigerator. I fol-
> low her, take out some milk, and pour it into a bowl, etc. That is communi-
> cation, a coordination of behavior. . . . Now suppose that one morning I
> don't follow the cat meowing. . . . If the cat were able to say, "Hey, guy, I've
> meowed three times, where is my milk?" that would be language . . . i.e.,
> communication about coordination.

Can you see this extra dimension of life? If you begin to see it, you
will soon realize how central it is to our existence.

Leo's Funeral

So let's look more into language as a phenomenon. Languaging, like all
behaviors or actions, is structurally determined. Humans are gifted with
certain innate structures in our brains and vocal apparatus that allow us
to generate words audibly. But, as with any other action, our languaging
behavior, and the fine-tuning of the structure that generates it, is also
shaped along the course of our lives.

For example, people of different nationalities may use the same word
to coordinate different actions proper to their particular cultures. I recently attended a funeral of my friend Leo, who belonged to the Armenian Orthodox church. For his family and relatives, a funeral was an
occasion of incense burning, chanting, and, after the service, a banquet
at an Armenian restaurant! For me, this kind of display was awkward,
unnatural, and unreal. In my world, a funeral consists of eulogies,
prayers, and tears—not a feast. The word *funeral* was the same for Leo's
family and me, but for them it brought forth a very different historic and
cultural reality—mourning through feasting.

Keep in mind that there is no such "thing" as a funeral, only the practices and standards that a group shares as symbolized by the word. This thought helped me to remember that Leo lived in a different cultural tradition than I did. This was part of his charm for me; he was refreshingly different. When I recognized this, I could better appreciate him in life, and his funeral, and I joined in the celebration of his life by eating heartily.

Our automatic languaging not only coordinates social phenomena, but it also may reveal our personal orientation toward others. For example, one of my patients was a particularly shy woman named Ellen. Once when entering the classroom, I accidentally bumped into her. Before I had a chance to apologize, she said, "I'm sorry." "Why apologize?" I replied, "I walked into you!"

I noticed during subsequent classes that Ellen apologized repeatedly, even when she raised her hand simultaneously with another participant. (Do you know people like Ellen?) I interpreted such automatic languaging as part of her orientation to living, deeply embedded in her structure. Each time she apologized, Ellen deepened her tendency to hold herself small and inferior. It was almost as if she saw herself as a walking interference in the lives of others. Her unawareness of this behavior allowed her to practice over and over again this act of self-diminution.

In the cases of Ellen and Leo, the act of languaging "I'm sorry" or "funeral" brought forth a special orientation to life—shyness and feasting, respectively. Language brings forth the world that you live in. If you want to change, it's profoundly useful to observe how you language yourself into being and in your relationships. Examples of this are all around us.

Buying a Coke

Living in language enables you to expand tremendously your repertoire of social interactions. When I ask a clerk in a local store in my Boston hometown for a *Globe,* I can be reasonably sure that I'll get what I want—a newspaper, not a spherical representation of the world. Giving me the newspaper is the right action to satisfy me. Moreover, I can assume that the clerk will give me today's paper and not last week's. This is also implied in the request. We share the same background, so the word "globe" produces the action that I want.

But there is a price for living in language with others—namely confusion and social breakdown when people do not share our history. For instance, if I ask for a Coke, things are less clear than when I ask for a *Globe.* I'm old enough to have grown up when there was only one Coke—the original Coke—and that's what I expect to get when I say "Coke." But nowadays there are several kinds of Coke. So it may take some clarifying conversations with a waitress before I get what I want. Or, conversely, if she simply assumes that she knows what I want, there is a chance of her bringing me Pepsi and producing a dissatisfied customer. Still, provided the waitress is attentive and she and I share the same background, I have a good chance of ultimately getting what I want.

Why Didn't She Ask Clearly?

But miscommunication about coordination can have more serious consequences than being brought the wrong Coke. My friend George recently told me a story about what happened to him after undergoing a routine physical examination. Three days after the exam, his physician, Dr. Lavine, phoned to inform him that a test of his prostate, the PSA, was abnormal. This could mean cancer. George was terrified. However, Dr. Lavine told George that a biopsy would settle the issue of cancer and guide his treatment plan. Dr. Lavine explained that he had already spoken to a urologist named Dr. Goldstein and that his office would be calling to set up an appointment.

Sure enough, within the hour Dr. Goldstein's secretary called. She said, "Be here next Tuesday. Be sure to arrive at nine. And bring your insurance card." These were her only instructions.

George had a worry-filled week. He called me several times for reassurance. I advised him that the biopsy probably would not show cancer, and that even if it did, it would be early cancer and therefore treatable. He was reassured, but just a little. Only the biopsy would set his anxiety to rest.

Finally the day of the biopsy arrived. George appeared at 8:45 at the office with his insurance card. "Let's get this over with so that I know if I'm well or not," he thought to himself as he was escorted to the small biopsy suite.

Soon Dr. Goldstein came in. He began by asking George several health-related questions, including what medicines he was on. George confided that he was taking Advil, a common medication that has a side effect of interfering with normal blood clotting. Dr. Goldstein told George that his taking Advil made the biopsy more dangerous by increasing the chance of bleeding. Because of this complication, the medication should have been discontinued for one week prior to the appointment. Unfortunately, Dr. Goldstein said, the biopsy would have to be postponed until next week. Then he added, "Didn't my secretary tell you about stopping this medicine?"

"Definitely not," replied George angrily. "She only told me to come on time and bring my insurance card, which I did."

Dr. Goldstein apologized and sent George out to the appointment desk to arrange for another visit. Now, George faced another week of worry, anxiety, fear, and restless nights.

This kind of breakdown is part of everyday experience. Someone gives us instructions or makes a request, we do what we heard, and the result goes sour. In this case, George was angry with the secretary and Dr. Goldstein. "You mean that I have to go through this worry for another week?" he complained to me. "I wonder if I should change urologists."

The mistake was an error of omission, but the result was serious: a frightened patient, one more week of suffering and worry, and a growing distrust of the physician and the medical system. Even though George's biopsy proved to be negative, poor communication had taken its toll. A month later, George was still upset about what had happened to him.

Many of you may have similar stories about confused encounters. It happens over and over again each day of our lives. Each time the result is dissatisfaction, frustration, and an erosion of trust.

Think of all of the times that you've had breakdowns with others that had their root in languaging. For example:

□ "You promised me and did not keep your word." In this breakdown, the requester has understood that the other person had promised to fulfill a commitment, and that he has not done so. This breakdown may leave the requester feeling betrayed and angry.

□ "Spicy Chinese food is good, I don't understand why you don't like it." People often have differences of opinion. "Spicy Chinese food is good" is not the "truth," even though the person saying it means it as such. "Spicy food is good" is the utterance of a person—his or her opinion, and only that. It is "true" only for him or her. Blindness to the fact that our judgments aren't universal truths can lead to arguments or the attempt of one person to dominate another with his or her opinion.

□ "The future is hopeless" is a statement that depressed people may make. They commit a linguistic error when they make such statements—speaking of the future as hopeless as if it were a fact, not a judgment. A depressed person's recovery, with or without medications, can be hastened by having them become an observer of their habits of languaging.

Linda, the Depressed Woman

Linda listened to this illustration of linguistic breakdown with fascination. "I say that hopeless line a hundred times each day. I awaken in the morning to a hopeless day, I have a hopeless husband, I'm hopeless about my career, I go to sleep without hope. Do you mean that each time I repeat this affirmation to myself that my chemistry changes?"

"I'm not sure, but I think so," I suggested.

My suggestion to you is that you join Linda and many others who have learned some of the fundamentals of languaging. When you learn you go through a common sequence, no matter what it is that you learn. First, you declare that something is missing, such as a good tennis swing or the ability to make fresh pasta. Here what is missing is our ability to be aware and effective in observing language. Then you find a coach, a book, or a teacher to help with your learning. Next, you either make a request of the teacher or begin to study the book in a mood of openness to learning. Behind your willingness to begin is the assumption that you can learn, and that the book or teacher will assist you. You trust your ability to learn. Finally, you listen (or read), practice, and correct—a universal cycle of learning, of building a new body for action. This sequence of learning is what I ask that you do here. The topic or domain for learning is language or linguistic behavior.

For the remainder of this chapter, I'll make more distinctions about language, many of which I learned from Fernando Flores. These distinctions will allow you to observe yourself and others in the act of languaging. The new distinctions can be powerful catalysts for making changes in your personal relationships, your family life, your job, and in your health.

Remember that you're dealing with habits. Like somatic or emotional habits, we have languaging habits. They have a life of their own. Don't expect miracles as you make observations about your "self-talk" and your conversations with others. As you increase your ability to observe yourself, new possibilities will be available to you.

Making It Simple

What if I told you that there were five and *only* five actions that you make in language? That would simplify your task a lot, wouldn't it? Well, it's true. When Fernando told me this I was amazed. "You've got to be kidding," I exclaimed. "So many words, and only five kinds of action!" Fernando explained that each class of words performs a different action, and each one is distinct from the others. Surprisingly, you already know these distinctions; you'll recognize them as I describe them. Let's look at each one in turn:

Requests

A request is an action that you take when you seek the assistance of another in satisfying an underlying concern that you have. You want something. A request is made in the present, at the moment you say it, but it invites a future action by another or others.

A request also involves a commitment on the part of the requester to be satisfied if the conditions specified in the request are met. If these conditions are met and the requester is not satisfied, the person fulfilling his promise may see the requester as manipulative, unfair, or demanding. He may say of the requester, "He's jerking me around. First he asks for something and when I do it, he's not satisfied!" (What mood would such an experience produce in you? In me it produces anger.)

Promises

A promise is what you speak to indicate your commitment to fulfilling what someone else has requested. It implies that you understand his or her request fully, and that you are competent and sincere about fulfilling what he or she has asked.

Trust is a very important judgment that we make about someone's rigor and sincerity as a promiser. When promises are not fulfilled and a person fails to take care of the consequences of the failure, the requester may feel betrayed or become resentful and begin to distrust that person.

What is important to see here is that the fundamental social action of trust lives in our assessment of others' sincerity, ability, and responsibility to keep their promises and commitments. Without trust, relationships, organizations, and societies are in a state of constant vigilance and chaos.

Declarations

A declaration is an utterance in which someone with the authority to do so brings something into being that wasn't there before. Can you imagine that! Language has the capacity to open a space of possibility for human beings. The Declaration of Independence is an example of this linguistic act. The United States was brought into existence when a group of men empowered to do so declared independence from England.

Of course, they had to back up their speaking by many other actions—fighting a war, setting up laws for the new country, etc. But with the declaration, the possibility for our country was created. Personal declarations such as "I will lose thirty pounds by July first" or "I will listen to my wife's concerns with more patience" have the power to shape our lives, if followed by consistent behavior.

The questions to think about around declarations are: Does the person have the authority to make this declaration? and What is this person's level of personal commitment to living his or her life in a way that will fulfill the declaration?

One of the most important of our personal declarations is the act of *forgiveness*. This crucial declaration is a commitment not to carry past resentment into the present and future. We are all human and make mistakes, sometimes egregious ones. People break their promises to us in ways that may cause us pain. The act of forgiving allows us to free ourselves from the burdens of guilt, anger, and resentment.

Forgiving someone doesn't mean that you are obligated to interact with him or her. You may or may not do that based on your assessment of whether you can build trust anew with that person and, of course, on your preferences. Trust allows us to live at peace in relationships, and forgiveness allows us to free ourselves from resentments and build life anew. Forgiveness is not forgetting—we remember. Hence, forgiveness is a stance that we must declare over and over again whenever resentment and anger arise.

Assessments

An assessment is a judgment that you make about the world in the interest of taking some action. For example, in the interest of going to a ball game, I might make the assessment "It's a beautiful day," in which no wind and a temperature of eighty degrees are my standards. On the other hand, in the interest of going sailing, my assessment "It's a beautiful day" means that the wind is blowing, the harder the better.

In both cases, the assessment "beautiful" implies first a statement for the sake of something (sailing or baseball); then a standard (e.g., no wind or twenty knots); and finally a judgment (beautiful or not beautiful). "A little beautiful" makes no sense.

Beauty as a quality is not in the day itself, but in the eyes of the speaker with the interests (the "for the sake of") and the standards. Often people argue over whether the day is beautiful, as if anyone with eyes could see what they see. *Assessments are never the truth.* They are statements people make that fulfill some concern with their particular standards.

As I write this, I can recall my daughter Rachel as a teenager protesting, "But my room *is* clean! See, all of my laundry is piled neatly on the floor." When she was a teenager, she had different standards of cleanliness from those of her mother and father. Part of living with a teenager—in fact, with anyone else—lies in the negotiation of standards for assessment.

Assessments are never facts, even though a lot of people may share the assessment. They are always informed by the interests and standards of the person making the statement. However, assessments may be grounded or not; i.e., there may be some evidence on which the assessment is based (in the case of a baseball game, the temperature of the day; in the case of sailing, the wind velocity). Rigor is related to the diligence and skill a person has in grounding assessments. A doctor, for example, is a person who has been schooled in making grounded assessments for the sake of improving patients' health. A lawyer makes grounded assessments for the sake of clients' interests under the law. See, it all happens in language.

Your historic narratives are assessments of yourself and others— "Others are smarter than me"; "You can't trust men"; "The future is hopeless." These assessments are generally ungrounded, but nonetheless determine what actions you will and will not take.

Pause for a few minutes and examine some of the automatic assessments that shape you. Think about age, money, race, physical appearance, health, and sex. What are the ungrounded truths that dominate and influence your life?

Assertions

An assertion is a statement you make for which you are willing to provide evidence. For example, if I say it is sixty-eight degrees in this room, I'm willing to show this to you on a thermometer. We live by the social agreement that this device reflects temperature. In other words, a society builds certain ways of establishing and asserting common, often quantitative, values—weight, length, height, time, I.Q., etc. These assertions live for us as "facts"; they are either true or false.

If you make an assertion and cannot provide proof, sometimes you have to withdraw the assertion. If you make an assertion contrary to or ignoring the evidence, then you are mistaken or lying.

Requests, promises, declarations, assessments, and assertions are the five basic building blocks of linguistic behavior. The concepts are simple, but it takes time for you to become a rigorous observer of breakdowns so that you can redesign your actions. It took me years to embody this material, and I'm still engaged in breaking old habits and developing more rigor. So don't expect to learn it all at once. Remember that learning involves structural alteration of your body. This takes practice and more practice. As you begin to look with these distinctions, you'll see more. As you see more, you can do more. Then you'll begin to embody these skills, and they will happen without conscious thinking. Be patient with yourself.

Communication Failures Cause Havoc

The fundamental challenge of relationships, guaranteed to produce miscoordination and conflict, is failure to listen. As I've said, communication in language between two people is communication between two biological beings who literally live in different cognitive universes. When you speak to another person, his or her system is triggered in unique ways that differ from how you would be triggered. When you speak, you are literally joining two worlds. Think of talking to a teenage daughter, a spouse while planning a vacation, or your manager during a performance review, and you can see what I mean. Two worlds can collide!

"Salt" was all my uncle Sam had to say at family dinners and everyone at the table jumped to find it. We did it to avoid another conversation where Uncle Sam would take a sip of his soup and yell at his wife, Rose, "My dear wife, Rose, when are you going to put enough salt in my soup?" Our structure, in each member of the family, had been altered so that we all shared a common understanding of the word *salt*. We avoided the flare-up that would inevitably follow by passing the salt. All he said was "salt"; we automatically heard the rest of the story.

This is not usually the case. When someone mentions "money," we each hear something different. One person may react by feeling, "I need more!" Another may hear, "It's the root of evil." Still another person may respond, "It can't buy happiness." Listening to another involves *listening to what your utterance meant to him or her,* not to you. When they speak, it means listening to more than just their words, but reaching for the concerns and understandings that underlie the words, as with Sam.

I was recently at my mother's hospital bedside the night before she was to have back surgery. When my mother's surgeon came in to give her a preoperative pep talk, he said to her, "I hope the operation works for you." Knowing my mother as I do, I realized the surgeon's comment would trigger uncertainty in her, which would lower her chances of successfully surviving the operation.

I asked the surgeon to step out into the hall. There I shared my concern. I asked him, "Go back in and tell her the operation will work. Try to elicit a strong placebo assistance for your work." (I'll explain the importance of this shortly.) The surgeon argued that he couldn't guarantee the operation. "Of course not," I said, "but she's not a doctor who would be offended if you made such a statement. You need to produce in her a sense of positive expectation." The surgeon considered what I said and returned to my mother's room. This time he told her the operation would work. I watched as my mother's face softened, her muscles relaxed, and she smiled. The surgeon had communicated effectively with her. He spoke to her concern, which I had helped him to listen to, and produced peace and hopefulness. In my mind, this effective communication was one of the reasons for the operation's success.

The cardinal sin of communication, which compromises all speech and relationship, is assuming that what was said is what was heard. To avoid this you must ask, observe, inquire, discuss, and listen for what the other person understands.

I call the common failures of communication the "Ten Linguistic Viruses." As I describe them to you, think of how you can use these common breakdowns and what you see in them as a platform for your listening. I call these breakdowns linguistic viruses because they attack relationships, alter the structures of the individuals in them, and cause dissatisfaction, bad moods, and even ill health. Learning what they are will allow you to listen to others more effectively, and heal them and yourself.

As you read each item, find examples in your life where you fall into the behavior I'm describing. Then, ask yourself what action you could take to improve the outcome for yourself and for others. This will guide your learning and healing. You will have more practice doing this in the exercise section that follows, but now is a good time to begin.

The Ten Linguistic Viruses

1. Not Making Requests

Often people think that there's something that they want or need from someone else, but they don't make a request. They may complain inwardly or to others but still they make no requests of the other party.

Why is this? One reason is that you may have a reticence or fear about asking others. They could say no to your request. This might be painful for you and cause you to feel rejected. In point of fact, a no to a request is just that—no to the action of requesting, not a rejection of the person. But that's what some of us hear.

Walter, the Angry Man

Walter said that he hates to make requests because "the SOBs just lie to you anyhow."

I asked him if he became angry when people said no to his requests. "Of course I don't," he said angrily.

I responded, "Walter, are you telling the truth about being angry? Maybe we should do a class check again."

He replied, "Okay, okay, it makes me angry. I hate to rely on people, they trick you and hurt you!"

"Are you sure that's true for everyone?" I asked. "Maybe you're a bad judge of trustworthiness." He grunted.

Another reason people don't make requests is that they're afraid others will think they're incompetent. They assume that they *should* do and know everything by themselves. Again, this is faulty thinking. Making a request is not an admission of weakness. Think for a moment about the president of the United States or the CEO of a large corporation. Think of the staggering number of requests that they make each day. In fact, one aspect of power has to do with the capacity to make powerful requests.

So, requesting doesn't imply weakness. A request simply invites another person to participate in your life. Take this as a way to honor others, not to burden them.

Still another reason people don't make requests is that they think a request is an imposition. Shy people especially have this orientation. They forget that one way that people achieve meaning in their lives is in fulfilling the requests of others. A physician feels satisfaction when she meets a patient's medical needs; a minister has meaning in his life when he brings spiritual vitality to his congregation. You show respect for people when you ask them to participate in your life through a request. Unfortunately, to our historically formed bodies, it may not look that way.

Linda, the Depressed Woman

Linda said that she never makes requests because "no one would want to help me."

I asked her why she was so intent on not having people experience the satisfaction of assisting her.

Linda replied, "That sounds backwards."

"Really?" I continued. "How do you feel when you do something wonderful for one of your children?"

Linda responded, "Happy, at least for a while."

"Then why are you not willing to give other people the privilege of helping you?"

She became both thoughtful and irritated. "You keep turning things around."

I acknowledged that it might look that way, but it was a serious question that I was asking. She agreed to think about it.

2. Living with Uncommunicated Expectations

One of the most common and pernicious forms of "not requesting" occurs when an individual lives in a world of "shoulds" and expectations that are really unexpressed requests.

Often we have private conversations with ourselves about what others should and should not do. But we never make overt and open requests of these people. Subsequently, when they don't do what we expect, we're disappointed, resentful, and angry. The other parties may not even know what was expected of them, or if they do they wonder, "What is she so upset about? She never asked me to do anything about this." "Shoulds" and expectations give no possibility for negotiation, declining, and satisfaction. They are setups for conflict.

3. Making Unclear Requests

"Well, I thought that's what you wanted. I tried." Well-intentioned people fail when they try to fulfill unclear requests. A lack of clarity in your request may have generated the breakdown. It's foolish to think that others should know what you want. Remember that others don't necessarily see the world as you do. To coordinate successfully, your requests must be precise and detailed. You're not insulting the listener if you make detailed requests. You're setting up the possibility for mutual satisfaction.

Of course, as you live with someone and build a history of coordination together, less and less detail is necessary. A surgeon at an operating table may just stretch out an open hand, and this means to the OR nurse, "Please give me a scissors of so and so type, closed, with the handle in my palm, right now." All of this is embodied understanding generated by years of working together.

When a new scrub nurse enters, holding out an empty hand may be an unclear request. The surgeon may need to give her detailed instructions in order to be satisfied. Making such distinctions is not an insult; it's an act of taking care of another in the search for mutual satisfaction. This caring leads to less stress, less anger, and more joyful collaboration.

Unclear requests also occur when you don't take the time to clarify what you want in sufficient detail to have the promiser understand what you want. You fire off a request and hope everything works out. If the other person accepts the request in this vague form and makes a promise to fulfill it, you both are set up for failure. You've left the promiser to guess what you want, and the promiser anxiously hopes that he's made the right guess. The danger is, of course, a communications breakdown with all its attendant negative consequences.

Here are some examples of unclear requests:

□ *Husband to wife: "I want you to support my career."*   Can you see that the husband may have an unclear or different picture than the wife of what support looks like? What kind of support? What actions? When? All of this is missing. Later on, when a minor problem arises, the maker of the unclear request is likely to say, "You promised to support my career, but you didn't!"

□ *Doctor to patient: "Get back to me if you don't feel better."*   The patient is left thinking, "Mmm . . . what does he mean by feel better?

And how much better? How long will it take to get better? Should I be worried if I'm not better by tomorrow? I don't want to bother him, but I'm confused." The unclear request leaves the patient anxious and feeling that the doctor doesn't care.

□ *Customer to waiter: "I'd like coffee."*   What is missing includes: iced or hot coffee? With dinner or after? With milk, cream, or black? If milk, what kind of milk?

Can you begin to see how aware you have to be when making requests to be certain that the listener hears what you want? Remember that when we request, we're joining worlds in action.

To achieve clarity pay attention to the following: What is it you really want? Does the other person understand what you want and when you want it?

Gretchen, the Perfectionist

Gretchen said that her mother never made clear requests of her. She always said, "You should know! If you studied the Bible, you would know God's way." But Gretchen rarely did know what her mother wanted and lived in dread of always being bad by doing bad. Gretchen's mother made unclear requests with the warning that if Gretchen didn't do as she asked she would be damned. Gretchen felt trapped, uncertain, and in danger—damned if she did, damned if she didn't.

---

4. Not Observing the Mood of Requesting

Some people make requests like demands. Or, conversely, they make requests like a beggar. When you do this, you fail to see that the mood of your utterance, as much as your words, affects the listener. If you're demanding, people might decline your requests because they see you as arrogant and righteous, or they might make promises to you out of intimidation, not choice.

Remember, coordinating action in life is like dancing in language.

For some listeners, the appropriate verbal dance is a salsa. For others, it may be a waltz or a march. Your objective is the result, not the style. So be aware. Watch the listener as you do your linguistic dance.

My high school algebra teacher was a big, intimidating man. He always made requests in the tone and mood of demands. Students rarely declined his requests, but acted resentfully when they tried to do what he had asked. Students would avoid being in his presence because of their sense of being trapped by his requests.

On the other hand, I had a patient named Shirley who made all her requests in the mood of begging. I always felt manipulated by her when she asked me to do something as simple as explain a concept in the course. She was so pathetic that I didn't want to make her suffer, so I promised what she requested so as not to feel guilty. Weakness and guilt—what a combination!

5. Promising Even When You Aren't Clear What Was Requested

Committing yourself when you aren't clear about what you've committed to is foolish. Sometimes a person thinks he knows what's being asked of him, so he begins an activity, such as making a meal. But as he goes along, his lack of clarity is revealed. He becomes confused. What did she really want? What if I'm doing it wrong? What do I do if she doesn't like the meal?

If this is the case, you can either go back and request clarification or plod on hoping that everything will work out. You may fail to notice that this state of "committed confusion" produces anxiety in you and, when you fail to produce the desired result, distrust in the other party.

For example, last year my accountant asked me to prepare a list of my business expenditures for my tax return. As I did, I discovered some large purchases of equipment. I asked myself, "Are these in the same category as travel expenses?" I guessed rather than asked my accountant. When I visited him, he said, "Matt, capital equipment is dealt with separately. I thought that you knew that." Because I didn't clarify his request, we had to waste time reworking the return, and we were annoyed with each other for the rest of the session.

If you're not sure what the requester wants, clarify it with him or her. You won't look stupid. Rather, you'll be building an identity of being committed to fulfilling his or her request.

Robert, the High Achiever

Robert said that he often made promises when he wasn't clear about what was wanted.

"I don't want to look stupid by asking," he said. "So I go ahead, hoping it will turn out okay and worrying all the time. This makes me tense and keeps me up at night."

"Robert," I asked, "could you actually be making yourself stupid by not asking?"

He looked puzzled.

I said, "When you don't ask, you never know whether you're doing what was requested or not. That must make you crazy and stupid. That's what I mean."

6. Not Declining Requests

Some of us say yes to every request. We've been trained to please other people, and this is made manifest in our compliance. We believe we're "good" people; we believe it's "bad" to say no.

The problem with this belief is that it's destructive for both you and others.

Let's look at yes-sayers first. They are often overloaded with promises to keep. There simply isn't enough time to do it all. The result is a perpetual fear of failure, which prompted the compliance in the first place. A vicious circle is established, which generates anxiety, burnout, and exhaustion.

Something else happens to yes-sayers—they end up doing a lot of things they don't want to do. They lose their right to live life by their own standards and declarations. Ultimately, they lose dignity and self-respect.

Things aren't much better for the people receiving the yes-sayers' promises. The promises all sound like yes. But there are differences. Some promises are authentically yes, but some are reluctantly yes. Requesters never know which promises will be fulfilled and which ones are in jeopardy. Over time, people become distrustful of the yes-sayer. They think, "You just never can be sure about him; he's not sincere."

The ability to decline requests is crucial for health and dignity. My patient Carol demonstrated this in a dramatic way. Carol had five young children, a husband, and a twelve-room house to care for. She also suffered from serious headaches. Her only moments of respite from the headaches were when she was admitted to the hospital. Subsequently, while in my course, Carol was doing an exercise in which her role was to say no. Almost as soon as she began, she abruptly stopped. Carol said that she couldn't say no, even in an exercise.

So we practiced. First she said no to one request. Then the next week Carol said no to two requests. And so on. Every time she got tense and couldn't say no, I asked her to breathe deeply and relax her muscles; then we would repeat the exercise. She practiced this exercise at home. Gradually her tolerance for saying no grew and she began to express this freedom at home.

By the end of the course, Carol reported that for the first time she had freedom in her life. She could now go into her bedroom and read. If her children asked for something, she could say no or "I'll do it later." She felt less tense and angry and her headaches decreased in intensity and frequency.

Linda, the Depressed Woman

Linda thinks that good people should say yes, so she always does. But she complains about the consequences of doing this. "It doesn't pay to be a good person. Other people take advantage of you. Then I get resentful and depressed."

I asked Linda if being resentful at everyone was what a good person would do. I suggested that there were only two possibilities for her—either continue her compliant behavior and remain resentful, or begin saying no when asked to do something she didn't want to do.

I added, "Can you imagine saying no in such a way that the other person doesn't feel rejected? Can you imagine taking care of another person in other ways?"

---

7. Breaking Promises Without Taking Care: Undermining Trust

I don't want to make this section sound moralistic, as in "Thou shalt not break promises." Rather, I want to show the human and biological consequences of a broken commitment to coordinate action.

When you make a promise, you're committing yourself to a future action and building expectation for that action in the other party. Trust is the assessment of the other person that you will fulfill your promise.

When someone says, "I trust you," he or she means, "I assess that you are sincere, competent, and reliable to do what you promised." When you trust someone—have a grounded assessment of his or her trustworthiness—you rest at ease and expect what was promised. If the promise is broken, you begin to lose trust in the person and feel betrayed.

We are all human and cannot know the future. In the process of fulfilling a promise, things may happen that keep you from completion. You may discover that you aren't competent to do what you thought you could do. Or you may fall ill. Still, the requester is waiting, counting on you.

If you ignore your promise and go on knowingly, you're consciously betraying your word and not taking care of the other party. When I do this, I feel awful. In contrast, if I contact the requester, describe the present problems that are keeping me from fulfilling my promise, apologize for the broken promise, offer to make a new promise in a time frame that I can guarantee, and assist with the cleaning up of any mess that I produced, we are both relieved. Our relationship can even strengthen from this mutually caring action, even though I didn't keep my promise.

Some people live in pervasive distrust of everyone, or a class of people—men, women, Jews, African-Americans, etc. My patient Betty didn't trust men because she'd been raised poorly by an alcoholic father who always broke his promises. But because she was so pretty, Betty was always attracting men. Each time the possibility for intimacy arose, she would end the relationship. Betty lived in an ungrounded assessment of distrust of all men. Assessment of individuals by their membership in a class rather than by individual actions is prejudice. Distrust sown by broken promises is a common prejudice and separates people of all races, cultures, and classes.

As you read these lines, remember a time when you didn't complete a promise. Notice any changes that this memory evokes. For me, thinking of an unfulfilled promise brings on a tension in my neck and chest that I call embarrassment or guilt. When I think of communicating this breakdown and making new promises to the other person, my body relaxes. See if this isn't the same for you. This is a linguistic way to take care of yourself and your well-being, and other people as well.

8. Treating Assessments as the Truth or as Assertions (Facts)

I remember Humberto Maturana saying, "Everything that is said is said by someone." His statement looks absurdly self-evident, but he was describing a deeper phenomenon—your judgments are a function of your history of living and the standards for satisfaction that you embody. There is no truth to your statements of judgment, just what you say. You can provide evidence for what you say, but that still doesn't make it the truth. On the other hand, an assertion is a statement about the world for which you can provide evidence. It is either true or false in this sense. Assessments are grounded; for assertions we must provide evidence.

If we treat assessments as the truth, conflict arises. For instance, Roz and I both love a "nice" home. For me this means a study, lots of bookshelves, a place for my stereo, and a quiet bedroom—very little about aesthetics or grandeur. For Roz, it means colors, textures, lighting, spaces, a sense of grandeur and flow and many other things that I don't think about or even understand. Can you imagine searching for a "nice" home together? We must blend, accept, and weave our truths.

Living with others in respect and dignity must include the idea that people have the freedom to have the standards they have. On the other hand, in marriage people must build shared standards for many things— where to live, how to educate their children, fidelity, and so on. Part of the process of marriage or any sustained relationship is building these shared standards and determining the domains in which each partner can have separate standards. Sometimes this even means sacrifice, but that's part of close sustained association.

Walter, Linda, Robert, and Gretchen

All of my patients saw something about themselves when I discussed treating assessments as the truth.

Walter said, "I'm usually right, and they're wrong."

Linda said, "They're usually right, I'm wrong."

Robert and Gretchen both agreed that the assessments of others made them crazy. For Robert assessments meant that he wasn't successful; for Gretchen the judgments of others meant she wasn't perfect and thus, in her mind, was a bad person. No wonder she was often defensive.

9. Making Assessments Without Rigorous Grounding

Even though your judgments aren't the truth, you can make them with rigorous "grounding": i.e., you can say what you say based on evidence. In a court of law, a verdict is an assessment—guilty or innocent. A jury makes these assessments after weighing the credibility of the evidence, or "grounding." Then they make a judgment. If they make the judgment for reasons of race, sex, ethnicity, etc., the judgment is not rigorous, it is prejudicial. (Such a conclusion will most likely be overturned by a higher court.) To avoid this, juries are carefully screened to eliminate prejudice. In addition, perjury, or the intentional provision to the jury of false evidence, is a criminal offense because it undermines the ability of a jury to make a grounded assessment.

What is important in the law is equally important in medicine. A medical diagnosis is only an assessment. To make this assessment, it must be carefully grounded by lab tests, an extensive medical history, a physical examination, X rays, and so forth.

Practitioners of disciplines other than Western medicine make assessments in different ways, collect other kinds of evidence, and have different standards. Acupuncturists have a system of meridians and energy. Chiropractors have a system of nerves and pressures. These assessments are neither right nor wrong, but should be judged by careful measurement of the results that they produce. Rigor is possible even in a world of uncertainty.

Linda, the Depressed Woman

Linda observed that she used to think that everyone's assessments were correct except hers, and that everyone knew better than she did. She reported, "I'm beginning to see that some people's opinions are useful and expert. Others are self-serving. I don't have to listen to everyone. I can choose."

10. Making Fantasy Affirmations and Declarations

When you make a fantasy affirmation and declaration, you assume that it will happen by itself. For example, a fantasy affirmation or declaration would be one like your desiring to start a restaurant, even though you don't know anything about cooking or how to run a business.

Powerful, intentional people do not indulge in fantasy affirmations and declarations. Their word is an embodied word, and they mobilize their life in pursuit of their goals. This does not mean that they are always guaranteed success, but their intent and direction is at one with their declarations.

An affirmation or declaration pictures a reality that does not exist yet, but is attainable through a series of reasonable steps. President Kennedy's famous declaration in 1962 was that America would put a man on the moon by the end of the decade. Although he didn't live to see it, we did accomplish what seemed like science fiction at the time of his utterance. His declaration was grounded in a rigorous appraisal of our country's scientific and technological capabilities.

Gretchen, the Perfectionist

Gretchen said that she had participated in a positive thinking course in which she made dozens of affirmations. She had no plan of action for any of them. She never fulfilled any of them.

My suggestion that involving her network of contacts to support her in reaching her goals seemed different and powerful for her.

"Then I could learn from others," she said.

Languaging and Well-Being:
The Viruses in Action

The Ten Linguistic Viruses not only create ineffectiveness and friction between people, but also produce negative mood states, which, in turn, threaten your well-being and health.

For example, people who never make requests usually don't get what they want in life and are often disappointed and stuck. Such people may have secret expectations of others, which they never express. This also leads to disappointment and anger and resentment. Inertia and anger are both negative mood states that produce body changes in the muscles, circulation, heart, and brain.

People who can't decline requests place their health in great jeopardy. They are often overburdened and become exhausted, burned out, and depressed. They become anxious, driven, or resentful and avoid people who might make requests.

Promising when you aren't clear what you've been asked is something you're likely to do when you don't want to look stupid or when you want to please someone. As the time grows near for completion of your task, your uncertainty grows. You become anxious and tense. Your anxiety may be reflected in jaw pain, bowel problems, or headaches.

People who hold their assessments as the truth are generally rigid or arrogant. They cannot stand diversity and become angry at differences. These people are a pain to be around and are themselves uneasy all of the time. Because they live in the shadow of "being wrong" they always insist on being right. "Type A" people often have this characteristic and are at greater risk for heart disease.

Robert, the High Achiever

Robert said that he was caught in a bind. "I have to be right all of the time if I'm to be a successful lawyer," he told us. "If I make a wrong assessment, I'm letting my client, my firm, and my family down."

For Robert, beginning to see an assessment as something that wasn't the truth but just a judgment began to open up something for him. He saw that he could make the best judgment possible, even consult with senior partners about it, but still know that even though he did the best he could, he still could be wrong. There was no truth. He found this unburdening, as if he had been seeking for something that didn't exist.

People who make assessments without rigor are viewed as flaky and full of opinions that change like the weather. They aren't taken seriously and they often suffer from insecurity and low self-esteem. Low self-esteem is a major risk factor for psychosomatic symptoms such as insomnia.

Gossip is an especially pernicious kind of assessment, which lacks rigor and purpose. People who gossip use assessments not as a basis of taking action, but as a basis for characterizing another person who is absent from the conversation. Gossips get a false sense of power from this activity, but underneath they remain insecure and uneasy. Gossip is a cancer to organizations and social groups.

If you take your promises seriously, not communicating broken promises can produce a sense of shame and guilt. Others begin to distrust you, and your public identity suffers. Your possibilities in life shrink. You go around depressed and have little energy to accomplish your goals in life.

People who don't make positive affirmations, or who make fantasy ones, live without meaning and purpose. Victor Frankl, a psychologist and philosopher, observed that during his concentration camp experience, people without meaning were vulnerable to the extreme conditions of life in the camps and perished. In contrast, people who had a purpose, generally one outside of survival, were sustained and lived. Part of the state of what we call depression is living a life of no possibility.

Robert, the High Achiever

Robert began to see that his declaration to become a successful lawyer was never anything that *he* made, but rather a declaration of his family and of his culture. He began to question its authenticity for him. It gave his life only passive meaning and was always a struggle.

In this section, we've begun to examine the ways in which your linguistic actions shape and create your interactions with others in the social domain and your orientation to the future. It should now be clearer that, literally, "you are what you say."

Further, it should be much clearer to you that linguistic actions have a profound affect on your life and your health. But what is the scientific explanation for how language does this? What is the interrelationship between language, thinking, and the state of the body that Fernando Flores discussed years ago at the Cronkhite Center? The answers to these and related questions lie ahead of us. The fact that we can't explain the association shouldn't deter us from applying this understanding. We used penicillin decades before we knew how it worked.

Words affect the body. The placebo effect shows this profoundly.

The Placebo Effect

When medical scientists set out to prove the efficacy of a new treatment or drug in human illness, they have to deal with what is called *the placebo effect*. This is the positive effect that an inert or inactive substance such as colored water will produce in a patient when presented as a "treatment." The magnitude of this effect is tremendous, especially with, but not limited to, more symptomatic or subjective complaints like depression, insomnia, or pain. Up to 40 percent of patients improve when given a placebo.

Because of this, investigators place "placebo controls" in their investigations to correct for the placebo effect. What a nuisance! Or so I thought in my med school days. Then, I was taught that the placebo effect was a sort of enemy of the well-intentioned scientist. Now, however, I realize that it shows the profound relationship between language and the body's physiology—a placebo changes expectation (a linguistic event). This in turn alters the body, just as the participants repeating Fernando Flores's affirmations in the seminar altered their moods.

Starting in the 1950s and continuing until this day, there is a renewed interest by the medical community in the placebo effect because of its prevalence. For a large part of human history, especially before the seventeenth century, most treatments administered to the ill were inactive. But many of them, if given well, greatly enhanced the placebo effect. Patients felt and often got better.

In his play *The Doctor's Dilemma,* George Bernard Shaw describes a Dr. Bonnington as follows: "Cheering, reassuring, healing by the mere incompatibility of disease and anxiety with his welcome presence. Even broken bones, it is said, have been know to unite at the sound of his voice."

So the placebo effect has not only to do with the substance itself, but with the substance administrator, often a doctor. In an essay on the placebo, pain expert Dr. Howard Brody says that the *meaning* of the placebo to the patient, and the interaction between the patient and the placebo giver, are the factors that generate the effects.

He cites three components of the placebo effect. First, there must be an understandable and culturally reasonable explanation of the illness. In medieval times, this may have been the assessment that there was an imbalance of humors, resulting from excess "black bile." Today this explanation would be nonsensical, and something like "You have a virus" would be more acceptable. But the explanation must be acceptable to the patient. The clinician or healer must explain the illness in a context that the patient can relate to.

Second, the caregiver must demonstrate care and concern. This undoubtedly affects the patient's mood in a positive way. The medicine is given in a context of caring. The patient responds by allowing himself or herself to be cared for.

And third, the intervention must be delivered with the strong expectation for the control or relief of the symptoms. Phrases that a physician uses to convey this include: "This will help," "I expect your symptoms to be diminished," or "I've found wonderful results in my patients with this treatment." If the patient trusts the physician, nature's remedy is unleashed.

Interestingly, Brody's three conditions for placebo enhancement are all linguistic acts. First, the explanation is a story that makes the symptoms make sense in the patient's cultural context. Second, the assessment of caring and concern is a linguistic act by a patient, encouraged by certain behaviors, as was the case with Dr. Bonnington. And third, the healer's expectation is a declaration of possibility made by someone with the authority and knowledge to make such a declaration and trusted enough to plant the seeds of hope when he or she says, "This medicine will bring you relief."

For our purposes, placebo effects are *real,* often manifesting in actual physiological changes in the body, and they are *linguistic,* embedded in conversations of cause, trust, and expectation.

Placebo treatment is not particularly effective with my dog Otto, since he doesn't have language. It wouldn't do Otto any good to tell him, "Many other dogs with your condition are helped by this pill." On the other hand, remember my mother's reaction when her surgeon returned to her room and painted a positive expectation of the next day's surgery? For a ninety-three-year-old woman to survive such major surgery is a testament to the power of the placebo effect and the power of words.

In a very real sense, you are what you speak—your identity, your possibility, the state of your body, and your health. This chapter is a start of your learning how to speak with awareness. Chapter 5 will help you learn how to listen to your moods and emotions.

EXERCISES

Major Points in Chapter 4

□ Humans live in language. Some animals have an elegant capacity to coordinate behavior, far greater than that of humans. Geese fly in flocks, fish swim in orderly schools. Humans, however, are the only species that can coordinate their behavior in language.

□ Human suffering is generated when we make the assessment in language that something is wrong or missing.

□ Planning, organizing, and change all happen in language. The Declaration of Independence, a declaration in language, made possible the "space" for the United States to exist. A marriage is created in language by the exchange of vows witnessed by a person authorized to oversee this set of mutual promises. Every contract is a set of actions in language.

□ Language doesn't describe an external reality; rather, it's an act of coordination between people who share the same background. A "beautiful" day for me is eighty degrees, no chance of rain, and no wind—good baseball weather. A "beautiful" day for going sailing with Roz includes a twenty-knot wind. The windier the better, or more "beautiful."

Beautiful is not *in* the day, it's for the sake of satisfying some concern of the speaker.

□ Since language is central to human life and you're already in it, you're more likely to live in peace and harmony if you know something about it. So in this chapter we make many distinctions in language. With these distinctions, you can better observe and design your own behavior, see your automatic traps, and redesign your actions.

□ There are only five kinds of actions that you can take in language. Once you learn them, you can observe these actions more effectively. Learning these distinctions is like learning golf—you go to a coach who instructs you largely by describing new distinctions (e.g., grip, backswing, position of the head, etc.) and by demonstrating those actions. In our dojo, I'll make distinctions about language and then you'll practice them.

□ The placebo response shows the power of language to alter your whole being, including your body. Presenting a medical intervention in a way that offers hope and expectation shifts the body in a positive way. Language acts have the power to alter the state of the body. You know this from everyday experience. If someone yells "Fire," your pulse rate soars and your breathing increases rapidly.

A Brief Check on Previous Learning

By now you're meditating at least ten minutes a day, and at least three to five days a week. Push toward this goal. Try to extend the time to twenty minutes each day.

Observe the automatic conversations that speak to you when you're sitting quietly. How do these conversations color your view of life when they arise? How do these thoughts affect your body? Then let the thought go and return to your breathing. Remember that meditation produces a subtle increase in self-awareness, and thus in personal freedom and power. Watch out for impatience, a reflection of our "fast-food" culture. Meditation is more than two thousand years old. It works.

Recall that in chapter 1, you began to observe yourself as a learner. Building practices for lifelong learning is essential for both personal satisfaction and health. How is it going? Are you encountering your habits as a learner and noticing them in real time?

In chapter 2, you focused on your body and learned that it was both the source and the shaper of your experience. Are you becoming more aware of your body? Are you seeing the moments and situations in which you're triggered? Keep looking.

And in chapter 3 you explored some of the major historical forces that molded and shaped you and your world. Are you becoming more aware of how your history has shaped your life?

Exercises for Reflection and Learning

You Are What You Say—Exercise One: the Elements of a Request

Miscoordination—either from requests that are not clearly made or not clearly understood by another person—is the cause of much human misery. When we don't get what we asked for from another or vice versa, we generally get upset. If we could learn to be more effective, both our productivity (our ability to produce satisfaction in others) and our general social mood would improve. In this exercise, you'll learn to identify the elements of a request. Knowing these distinctions can save you and those around you a lot of grief.

Look at the following example to see how this works.

Father to his son: "Jim, please go to the drugstore and buy me a *Globe* and bring it back before breakfast."

ELEMENTS OF THE REQUEST:

Speaker: Father

Listener: Jim

Shared understanding(s): Both understand what a drugstore is. Both know what a *Globe* is (Boston newspaper). Both know when the usual breakfast time is.

The speaker will be satisfied if: Jim brings back today's paper before breakfast.

By when: Before breakfast.

With a shared understanding of these key elements, Dad and Jim have a good chance of producing mutual satisfaction—Dad gets the newspaper, and Jim receives good-guy points.

A request is incomplete without both parties having the same understanding of each of these conditions. If they don't, it's like two people playing a game with different rules—chaos and conflict are sure to follow. I'll have more to say about this later, but first let's practice identifying the elements.

REQUEST EXAMPLE ONE

Recently I said to my niece, "Sarah, please go to the Registry of Motor Vehicles today and get me a resident parking sticker."

See if you can identify the shared understandings that fulfillment of this request hinges on. Identify the elements of this request.

ELEMENTS OF THE REQUEST:

Speaker:

Listener:

Shared understanding(s):

The speaker will be satisfied if:

By when:

Can you begin to see the possibility for a breakdown if my niece and I understand one or more elements differently?

What happens to my mood or Sarah's if she produces something other than what I thought that I asked for?

Your Response:

What's Sarah's reaction when she thinks she's doing what I wanted, but then I say, "No, you're not!"

Your Response:

Much human conflict in day-to-day life has its roots in this kind of mis-coordination. If Canada geese were so miscoordinated, they would collide in midair. We collide emotionally. What works is being sure about what you want, and then having a conversation with the other person to see if the two of you understand the same thing. This is emotional preventive medicine.

REQUEST EXAMPLE TWO

Recently my wife, Roz, said to me, "Matt, please pick up some flounder and broccoli at the market for dinner tonight."

Again, identify the elements. Who is the speaker? Who is the listener? What situation will satisfy my wife? By when? What shared understanding is assumed by the request?

ELEMENTS OF THE REQUEST:

Speaker:

Listener:

Shared understanding(s):

The speaker will be satisfied if:

By when:

Can you see the confusion that would result if Roz and I don't share the same understanding? I know, for example, that Roz wants about one and a half pounds of fresh fish for the two of us, not six pounds of frozen fish. I also know she wants fresh, not frozen, broccoli. Additionally, I know that we eat at six-thirty. So I must have the food in our kitchen by six at the latest. If I were uncertain of her conditions, I would be irresponsible to merely guess and hope that it turned out. Do you ever do that in relationships, with children, at work, with friends?

You Are What You Say—Exercise Two: Missing or Confused Elements

Sometimes you want to make a request, but your lack of clarity and care in speaking virtually guarantees a communications breakdown. Remember, the listener's effective listening is critical for successful communication.

Here are some examples of this problem. See if you can observe the elements that are missing or confused. Then, write them down.

1. Mother to daughter: "Please clean your room."

Missing elements (Hint: clean for a teenager and a mother are not the same):

What else is confused or missing?

2. One friend to another: "You know, Charlotte, this is a difficult time for me. I want your support."

Missing elements (Hint: support is not an action):

What does she really want?

What else is missing?

3. A physician to a patient: "Call me if things change."

Missing elements: (Hint: change how? change what? how much?):

What else is missing?

4. A customer to a painter: "John, I want this room painted pale pink."

Missing elements:

5. Mother to grown child: "It would be nice if you would call sometimes."

Missing elements:

Return to each of the situations and ask yourself what action the requester could have taken to avoid possible communication breakdown. In each case, the person making the request caused the other person to take some action even though the request was unclear. But in these cases, as in life, what resulted was not mutual satisfaction and the joy of having worked well together. What resulted was uncertainty, anxiety, guilt, irritation, even anger and resentment.

When breakdowns occur over and over again, distrust and isolation develop. People stop asking for help and become resentful, feeling that they have to do everything themselves.

We'll go into this further in the next exercise. For now, review the elements of a clear request and make some notes about what you learned about yourself and your habits in coordinating with others. Remember, we make requests all the time anyhow. Now you're beginning to see the actions more clearly and can be more precise, more effective, and more caring.

Notes About Yourself as a Requester

Keep returning to this exercise daily at first, then periodically. As you do, you'll see more and more about this fundamental action of human coupling and more about the identity that you produce in relationships. What many people see in doing this exercise is that making clear requests has profound effects in their lives. They also see that they have fallen into certain habits to avoid clarity, to avoid seeming bossy, or to avoid requesting at all costs. Make this exercise a practice.

When they see this and begin to take new action, others take them more seriously. They take themselves and their needs more seriously. When you make really clear requests and promises, people perceive that you really care, not that you are pushy. Listen to your habits of requesting.

You Are What You Say—Exercise Three: Analysis of a Breakdown

We ask for something, the other person acts but doesn't produce what we want. If this happens repeatedly, it has practical consequences in our relationships.

When you become aware that your request hasn't been fulfilled, you may have an emotional reaction such as anger, or mistrust, or anxiety. On the other hand, a breakdown is an opportunity to analyze what went wrong in the coordination between request and fulfillment. You can thus use these difficult moments to *strengthen,* not erode, your relationships as well as your communication skills.

During the day, when you have a breakdown in your coordination with others, jot down the details on a card, in a notebook, or in a computer file. In the evening, record at least three breakdowns in the space provided below.

COMMUNICATIONS BREAKDOWN ONE

Story:

Your emotional reaction to the breakdown:

Potential consequences of the breakdown:

Elements missing for effective communication:

To avoid this breakdown, I could have:

COMMUNICATIONS BREAKDOWN TWO

Story:

Your emotional reaction to the breakdown:

Potential consequences of the breakdown:

Elements missing for effective communication:

To avoid this breakdown, I could have:

COMMUNICATIONS BREAKDOWN THREE

Story:

Your emotional reaction to the breakdown:

Potential consequences of the breakdown:

Elements missing for effective communication:

To avoid this breakdown, I could have:

After you've finished analyzing the three breakdowns, speculate on the health consequences for you of recurrent miscoordination with others.

Possible Health Consequences for Me of Miscoordination:

Now, speculate about your weaknesses in requesting and promising that could cause recurrent breakdowns.

Habits I Have That Lead to Recurrent Miscoordination:

If you have noted the health consequences of miscoordination and observed some of your habitual behaviors that generate breakdowns, you've found a powerful new way to improve your health—the rigorous design of coordination of your relationships with others. Altering a bad and risky habit is the nature of true preventive medicine. That is what you can do here.

We've just begun to scratch the surface of learning linguistic distinctions, but I promise you that if you develop competence in this area, you'll have more satisfaction in your life, which will in turn enhance your wellness.

You Are What You Say—Exercise Four: Declining Requests

Some of us have trouble saying no. Because you want to be nice, pleasing, and good, you say yes and end up doing lots of things you don't want to do. This erodes your self-respect. In addition, you come to resent the people who made the requests—sometimes it even makes you break your reluctant promises.

Such passive compliance with others can produce moods dangerous to your health—moods of anger, or resentment, or helplessness.

Your inability to say no is not a problem of articulation or diction, but of an *embodied tendency* to have to say yes, to be "nice," and not to upset others. Learning to say no requires practice for those "yes-sayers" who find it difficult. Remember, saying no is not better than saying yes. But if you can't say no when you mean no, you put yourself and others at red-alert-relationship-risk. Learning to say no with dignity is a "linguistic vitamin"—an action in language that is necessary for health.

One last point. You can say no to a request and still take care of the other person. You can offer alternatives or agree to do part of what is asked. Your goal is to give the listener the sense that his or her request has been declined, not that he or she, the person, has been rejected.

Now for the exercise: Sit down in a comfortable chair, close your eyes, and recall a situation when you promised to do something that you didn't want to do. Picture that situation in detail: the people, the place, how you acted, how they acted, etc. Recall how you felt in your body as you made this promise that you really didn't want to make. Was this an old feeling?

Note briefly what you observed.

Notes:

Close your eyes again and imagine this situation one more time. Really get into it and let your old feelings arise. See yourself on the verge of promising to do something that you don't want to do, but this time, imagine yourself saying, "No, I will not do what you request" in a mood of respect. Say, "But out of my concern for you, I can do such and so as a substitute. And in the future, if you have other requests, feel free to ask me." Actually imagine yourself declining the request in this respectful way. This is not assertiveness training based in anger and pain, it's relationship training based in love, caring, and dignity. Practice a variety of ways to decline respectfully, e.g., "No, I'm sorry, I just can't." "No, I'm afraid not, but thanks for asking." "Sorry, I wish I could help you, but I can't this time."

What does this feel like in your body? What consequences could developing this ability have for your health? For your self-respect?

Begin to observe yourself in daily life when others make requests of you. See if you can recognize any conditioned linguistic tendency to be a "good" person and say yes at the expense of your autonomy. Or if you automatically tend to do the opposite, to decline. Just seeing how you embody these habits will begin to give you freedom to choose.

While you're learning to be a new observer of yourself, you may find that you continue to say yes to requests by others that you don't want to do. Remember, you're building a new body for being in the world with others. This takes time and practice. Eventually, you'll get there. Take notes on what you observed in this entire exercise.

Notes:

You Are What You Say—Exercise Five: Making and Receiving Assessments

We need the assessments of others for our own learning, especially the assessments of those who know what we don't, assessments made with rigor, with evidence—what I call grounding—and with our interest at heart. This is how we learn from others.

Unfortunately, most people listen to the assessments of others in a way that makes learning difficult. When people assess us, we act as if they're stating a good or bad "truth" about us. And our bodies react in a defensive or embarrassed way.

A more biologically sound and accurate way of listening would be to regard the person making the assessment and remind yourself that "he is the observer that he is, which is based on his history. He has certain eyes through which he views the world. With these eyes he has made the following assessment. *His assessment is not the truth, but it could be useful.*" Notice that it probably took the reading of this entire book to this point for you to see the accuracy of this statement. It really is so. Everything that another person says is a product of what he or she sees, what his or her history allows him or her to see. It's not the truth, but it may be very, very useful if we can hear it.

It's critical for your health and for your learning that you listen to the assessments of others as *their opinions shaped by their history,* and not the truth. If you do, you can learn from them. You can honor and respect their opinions. Without this ability, you'll be in a constant struggle over who is "right" and who is "wrong."

Developing this ability takes practice. Begin with this exercise:

□ Do this exercise with someone close to you who you trust.

□ Sit down facing each other. As you enact the exercise, observe your mood, your body postures and reactions, and your manner of speaking.

□ Ask the other person to make one assessment after another about your clothes. They may be positive or negative judgments. But ask the person to keep making them for a full minute. Listen to the assessments but keep observing what your body does at the same time.

□ After one minute, stop and have a conversation with your partner. What is he or she seeing? What is behind these judgments? Does he or she have different standards than you do? What can you learn from him or her?

□ What did you see about your body when receiving assessments? Most of us are triggered tremendously by the assessments of others.

□ Do you feel these body changes impact your health? Your learning?

Continue this exercise, but ask your partner to assess you in other areas: your intelligence, your competence at your job, your ability in parenting, your appearance, your trustworthiness, etc.

As you do this exercise, keep listening for the other person's standards and for what he or she sees. Many trying this exercise experience a natural tendency to request information and teaching from the other person. When we break the barrier of assessments being the "truth" and remember that they are personal judgments, made by another person, a space opens for learning, sharing, and asking. The "right-wrong" game and its social and physical consequences begin to dissolve. Take notes about what you see about yourself in receiving assessments.

Write Briefly on Each of These Questions:

Do you have difficulty making and delivering assessments to others?

Do you have difficulty receiving assessments?

What happens to your body when someone is assessing you?

Speculate about the consequences in your life of seeing assessments as the "truth."

Notes

Building a body that can make and receive assessments is critical for health, learning, and self-respect.

You Are What You Say—Exercise Six: From Complaining to Requesting

At different moments in your life, the actions of another person, or some situation, may not please you or satisfy your concerns and cares. You can either complain about this or take action by making requests of others.

Do this exercise with a colleague at work, a friend, or a family member. Warn him or her before you begin that you are doing an exercise to see the difference between complaining and requesting and how each influences your relationship with that person.

□ Pick something about that person that doesn't suit you. Complain about it for thirty seconds. Complain emotionally and verbally. Let him or her know how much you suffer with what he or she does.

□ Now stop and take some deep breaths to get settled. Invite your partner to do this as well. This may take a minute or so.

□ Then share with each other what it felt like giving and receiving the complaints.

□ As a result of the complaining, did anything new happen?

Now for the second part of the exercise.

□ Pick the same topic with the same person.

□ Make a clear request (remember the elements of a request).

□ Give him or her the chance to promise to do what you requested, or think about it, or decline.

□ Now, share what the experience is for each of you for requesting instead of just complaining. What new possibilities arose?

I told you earlier that I'm not giving advice in this book, but here I'll break that rule, one time. *You will suffer less the more that you convert your complaints into requests.* So will other people around you. Instead of saying, "I hate it when you make so much noise," try asking, "Could you please stop tapping your pencil on the table while you're reading the newspaper? It's distracting to me." Be sure, however, to grant the other person the freedom to decline. Converting complaints to requests is a major support of a healthy lifestyle.

Take notes on what you see about yourself complaining and requesting.

Notes

You Are What You Say—Exercise Seven: Promising with Care

When we make a promise, or receive one from another, we're committing ourselves to a future action together. Each party's expectations are based on this exchange of vows. Trust is the glue that keeps us together until the act is performed. Trust involves the belief that a person will take the actions necessary to fulfill his or her promise.

We consider people trustworthy if we can count on them. When someone breaks a promise, we call that betrayal. We become irritated or angry when this happens. What we expected did not occur; our life is in some sense disrupted.

But why would a person break a promise? The most common reason is that he or she didn't understand the request in the same way the requester did.

Another reason is that the person was unable to do what was necessary to fulfill the promise, either because he or she lacked the necessary knowledge or skills or because there was more involved in executing the promise than the person thought. This is a common occurrence. Still a third reason a person may have chronic problems delivering on promises is that he or she may intend to keep his or her word, know what to do, but can't get organized to do it. He or she isn't reliable. A final reason someone can fall down on the job is that he or she never intended to fulfill his or her promise in the first place.

If others continually break their word, their relationship with you suffers. The same is also true of your relationship with others.

In the following exercises, use the distinctions that I made above to observe promises that you have made and others have made to you, and what you did when these promises weren't fulfilled. Write these observations down.

EXERCISE ONE IN PROMISING

Recall a specific time when you made a promise, took the action, and then were told that what you did wasn't what was requested. What were the consequences? What could you do to avoid this situation?

YOUR RESPONSE

EXERCISE TWO IN PROMISING

Recall a time when you made a promise, began to work on it, and found that you didn't know how to do what you needed to do. What were the consequences? What did you do?

YOUR RESPONSE

Remember, sometimes we have to revoke promises.

EXERCISE THREE IN PROMISING

Recall a time when you made or someone made to you a promise that they had no intention of keeping. What were the consequences? Do you respect this action? Would you ask them to promise again? Would someone ask you to promise again?

YOUR RESPONSE

Remember that promising is about relationship and expectations. If you can't fulfill a promise, communicate this to the other party. Then either revoke the promise, make a new promise, or apologize. Don't ignore the situation. If you do, you are really ignoring the other party, which is profoundly disrespectful.

When you don't fulfill your promises, you'll feel guilty; when others don't keep their promises to you, you'll feel let down and angry. Promising with rigor and carefully managing breakdowns builds your identity in a positive way and establishes a network of trust and loyalty around you.

Notes on Promising and Trust

You Are What You Say—Exercise Eight:
Automatic Writing

Review your notes on the exercises. Then write for three to five minutes (or more if you like) on what you see about yourself and others in languaging—i.e., making and receiving requests, declining requests, making and receiving assessments, complaining, etc. Observe your history in the light of these linguistic habits and their consequences. What new actions do you commit to learn?

Automatic Writing

Automatic Writing

As I said before, human beings live in "a house of language." You are languaging all the time. Your social life, your social identity, the self that you know are largely woven through your languaging. In these exercises, I've given you some distinctions necessary to begin to observe yourself and others in action. The exercises may seem awkward and artificial. Think of them like going to the gym. Lifting weights is awkward, but it strengthens you for meeting your concerns in life. The same is true here. This chapter is a linguistic gymnasium. Keep doing these exercises until they reveal themselves in changes in how you act in daily living.

The Experiences of My Patients in Doing These Exercises

Gretchen, the Perfectionist

Gretchen never declined the requests of others. Her rule was to always say yes. As a consequence, she often found herself overburdened and anxious at work. When in this state, her stomach would give her trouble.

When Gretchen did these exercises, she realized more clearly than ever that she had lost her sense of autonomy and self-respect. This had caused Gretchen to resent and avoid contact with people. Her circle of friends was limited. Her social life was minimal. She saw people as too "demanding."

Gretchen never made assessments of others because she feared that they would find her judgmental like her mother. Also she feared that she could be wrong. In the assessment exercise, she saw that "if I offer my judgments as *only* my judgments, then I can be of more help to people." She continued, "My mother never conditioned her judgments with this understanding. I always felt that her judgments were the truth, and so did she."

Walter, the Angry Man

Walter always became furious when people broke their promises to him. But when he did these exercises, he saw that he often assumed that others had made promises to him even when they had not. Walter noticed, for example, that he became angry when someone would blow a car horn, even though there was obviously no broken promise. He had rigid expectations of most people and their noncompliance with his expectations was the source of his almost continual anger.

Walter never made requests of others because "they won't keep their promises anyways." He lived in this narrative. "No wonder I think I have to do everything myself," he said. Nobody ever dared to make an assessment of Walter out of fear of his anger. The views of others weren't available to him. He said, "When someone else gives me their opinion, it feels like I'm wrong and bad; I have to protect myself."

In these exercises Walter began to see the shell of social armor that he had built around himself and how it hurt him, rather than served him.

Robert, the High Achiever

Like Gretchen, Robert said yes to every request. He believed that a "nice boy" like him should please people and not say no. As a result, Robert often found himself overburdened.

Robert wasn't bothered by some negative assessments, such as when someone said he wasn't a good athlete. On the other hand, Robert became defensive and argumentative if someone assessed his intellectual or professional activity negatively. His self-esteem centered on his intellectual achievement. The opinion and advice of others in this area drove him crazy. The consequences of this were tremendous. First, he felt it necessary to place himself in "safe" situations rather than risk doing something new. Also, he avoided having his work critiqued by experienced lawyers. "I just can't do it," he told me. As a result, his learning was slowed down dramatically at this point in his career.

In class, Robert acknowledged that there was something very important in seeing that assessments were just assessments, not facts. But he doubted that such knowledge would help him. I suggested, "Keep practicing making that distinction in real life, and report back."

"I almost never make requests of others," Robert said. He believed that if he did make requests, especially at work, others would think him incapable. This added to his already overburdened state. Robert felt he had to do everything himself, which meant he'd have to stay at work until 10:00 P.M. most nights. This had a tremendous impact on his family life and his health. Robert didn't get adequate rest. His life was out of balance.

"I never thought that making a request of others could be seen as honoring them," Robert commented.

"Yes," I said. "It makes them feel special."

Linda, the Depressed Woman

During this exercise, Linda also saw that she never made requests of others. "Who am I to have other people go out of their way?" she said. As a result, Linda never asked anything of her husband and children. She shouldered the burdens of a large family with resignation and suffering. This caused her to be exhausted most of the time.

Linda also saw that the assessment that she was stupid and ineffective pervaded her life. When I asked her about the grounding for this assessment, she looked puzzled. Linda replied, "That's the way it is; that's what everyone, including me, thinks."

"What is the evidence that you're totally ineffective?" I asked.

Linda became thoughtful. "Well, I *am* a good mother, and a fine cook," she said. "And also an expert knitter as well. I guess that I'm not stupid about everything. I never thought of myself this way."

I commented that what she said was true for most people—they knew what they knew and didn't know what they didn't know. "Stupid is an ungrounded assessment, and you've let it run your life," I said. Linda became teary-eyed as she saw this clearly.

Five Linguistic Vitamins for Health and Well-Being

Linguistic Vitamin One: Make clear requests.
Linguistic Vitamin Two: Decline with respect and dignity.
Linguistic Vitamin Three: Listen to assessments as assessments, not as the truth.
Linguistic Vitamin Four: Convert complaints to clear requests.
Linguistic Vitamin Five: Promise soundly and take care of broken promises.

Chapter 5

Reasons of the Heart

When I am a brainiac [filled with bad thoughts about David's death] I feel terrible, but when I am quiet in my heart I feel fine.
  —USHA McCLELLAND, shortly after the death of her father, David

Detachment doesn't mean you don't let the experience penetrate you. On the contrary, you let it penetrate you fully. That's how you are able to leave it.
  —MORRIE SCHWARTZ, from *Tuesdays with Morrie*

Moods and emotions are the spice of life, providing its colors and vibrancy, its joy and sorrow, its enthusiasm and grief. Moods determine what you're likely to do and what is difficult for you to do. In a mood of joy, it's easy to sing a happy song; in a mood of depression, it's hard to plan a party. Additionally, moods are a major determinant of your well-being and your health. Negative moods twist and distort your body, your physiology, and your chemistry in ways that I'll describe below.

Moods and emotions permeate every aspect of your life, yet you live as if you have as little control over them as the weather. People describe their circumstances in life from a body already possessed by moods. Conversely, people talk about how the world alters their moods, blaming them on God, bad luck, their spouse, etc.

As a physician, I often see the impact of moods. For example:

☐ Lois, a healthy forty-seven-year-old businesswoman, had a terrible and violent argument with her business partner over their company's future. She left work in a mood of despair. That night she had a heart attack at home and died before reaching the hospital.

☐ Charles, fifty-four, developed sexual impotence when he separated from his wife. For many months he lived in a mood of hopelessness. When they reached a divorce agreement, Charles's sexual function returned.

☐ My father battled pancreatic cancer for six pain-racked months. On my mother's eighty-fifth birthday, he insisted on sitting at the dining table with the family. Because of the happiness of the occasion, my father was in a mood of joyfulness. That night he ate the heartiest meal that he'd had in months, laughed fully, and told us that he had no regrets about his life. He died the next morning.

Richard Lazarus, a leading psychologist in the area of mood and emotion, explains what's at work in these examples:

> I suggest that moods have to do with the larger background of one's life, which feels either troubled or trouble free, negative or positive. A good or bad mood, whether or not it has a distinct provocation, depends on how one is doing in the agendas of one's life overall.

So, your moods are your body's manifestation of how you're doing in the areas of life that concern you; at the same time, the moment-by-moment state of your body mirrors, or should I say is at one with, your mood or emotional state.

Reynell, a patient, demonstrated how much control you can have over your moods.

Reynell's Gift

One morning at my clinic, I received a call from Reynell, a thirty-three-year-old woman who informed me she had end-stage breast cancer. She had called me because she had heard that in my practice I focused on the whole person. As we chatted, Reynell told me that she was married to an investment banker named John and had a seven-year-old son named Brian. They were a close and loving family. Reynell then made a startling request of me. She wanted my assistance in giving John and Brian a great gift—the gift that she should die with dignity and at home.

As Reynell spoke, I had to force myself to listen and not be flooded by my own emotions. This was a very big request. Before I made the commitment, I agreed to see her that afternoon.

I arrived just before five o'clock. As I approached her residence, I could easily understand part of her request. She lived in a large, Tudor-style house on a lovely tree-lined street. I rang the doorbell, and after a couple of minutes Reynell opened the door. "Dr. Budd, I presume," she said with a bright smile.

She was a pretty woman of medium height, with a sharp nose, prominent green eyes, and blond hair pulled back from her face. Over a night-gown, she wore a dark blue bathrobe, grown too large for her wasted frame.

We walked to her kitchen and sat down. The kitchen was a product of Reynell's imagination. The room was bright and airy, the windowsills were lined with plants, and the walls were festooned with landscape paintings drawn by Reynell—she was an artist, it turned out. She had even made the table and chairs we were sitting on. As we talked, I was struck by Reynell's sincerity in wanting to end her life in a way that would help John and Brian heal from the devastating loss that would come shortly. "I think there's little to gain," she said, "by spending my last days in a hospital. I love it here."

That being said, I agreed to help her. Together we devised a plan to meet Reynell's medical needs. She wanted no further chemotherapy, but she asked to be as pain-free as possible while remaining conscious and relatively alert. I told her I knew an expert in pain management who would help me devise a combination of medications that would have the best chance of obtaining these goals.

Reynell had a second request—that I visit with her periodically and "just listen" as she gave voice to her fears, her feelings, and her pain. I promised her I would. What she meant is exactly what I described in chapter 4 as listening—listening to her, not my interpretations of her, as much as I could.

I didn't anticipate how hard honoring this request would be for me. Years of medical training had made me into a problem-solver, a doer. In order to "just listen" I had to step outside of my professional self and "be" with her. As time went on, I got better at doing this. Reynell was a good teacher. She would remind me that "there is nothing to fix" and returned me continually to my promise. I began to find this new role satisfying in a way that I hadn't expected. My generous and concerned presence was comforting, and it had nothing to do with my medical knowledge.

Over the next few weeks, Reynell became weaker. One day, when I made my customary visit, I was greeted by John and Brian. Also present were two friends—one who played the guitar, the other the flute. Reynell explained that it was rehearsal time for the hymn that she wanted to be played as she died! I had never experienced anything like this before. For the next half hour, all of us, including Reynell, practiced "Amazing Grace," her favorite song. Following the rehearsal, Reynell and I met for one of our listening sessions. I adjusted her pain medications and left. Each time that I "just listened" to her, she would end the session by saying, "You helped a lot." This amazed me, because in my entire education, helping was equated with doing and fixing, not just listening.

The next morning John called and asked me to come quickly—Reynell had told him she was dying. I raced to their house. When I entered their bedroom, I was struck with how beautiful Reynell looked. She wore a white lace nightgown and her braided hair was adorned with two white flowers. Only her yellowed skin and labored breathing indicated the portentous moment. She greeted me with a warm but very feeble smile that told me her mood was alert and peaceful even though her body was failing.

Reynell then beckoned to her husband, son, and musician friends to draw near. She tenderly but emotionally squeezed each of our hands in thanks. While holding John and Brian's hands, she asked us to sing. Music filled the room. Our voices did not betray a hint of the heartbreak we felt. Toward the end of the song, she closed her eyes and died.

We stood by her bed for what seemed to be an eternity—it was only a few minutes by the clock. We wept and hugged one another. After a while, I performed the rituals that a physician must do—calling the coroner, filling out the death certificate, etc. As I did, I felt connected to the three-thousand-year-old tradition of being a doctor in a way I never before had. Yet I had done very little "medicine." I had a new sense of myself as a doctor.

Over the next few months, I saw John and Brian from time to time. Of course, they grieved deeply for their lost wife and mother, but always with the deepest love and respect for her. Reynell's dignity and courage served as an inspiration in their recovery. Brian has done well—he's now a medical student and is happily married. John took off from his job for four months to grieve. Several years later he remarried.

Reynell was an important teacher to me. She showed me that listening was as powerful as telling and that supporting others was as important as a prescription. These were lessons taught to me in my youth by Jackson Rice, the family physician, but ones that I had forgotten.

Most importantly, Reynell demonstrated that Richard Lazarus was correct—moods are connected to one's interpretation of the circumstances in life. Inside the interpretation of a "terrible thing has befallen me," Reynell could have been angry and depressed. But inside of the interpretation "a terrible thing is happening to me. Now is my chance to leave a legacy of inspiration, acceptance, and dignity to my family," she produced a very different mood and a way of being. The dignity she displayed sustained her grieving family after her death.

Although Reynell provided me with an example of the power a person can have over her moods, I wondered if any scientific evidence showed a connection between mood and actual physical pathology or healing. Further, I was curious if control over moods could affect physical healing as it did emotional healing in Reynell's case. As I reviewed the medical literature, several experiments took on a new meaning for me.

Preoperative Care

Henry Beecher was a famous professor of anesthesiology at Harvard Medical School. He was the first to describe so-called battlefield anesthesia, a situation in which in combat, soldiers may not even recognize or feel a major wound because of their emotional state. They keep fighting as if nothing has happened to them. Only later, or when someone points it out, does the soldier know that he's wounded. Any parent has seen battlefield anesthesia. When a child falls, she is stunned and motionless, but not in obvious pain. Only when she sees her parent frantically running toward her does she begin to cry.

In the early 1950s, Beecher continued his research into the phenomenon of the effects of emotion. In one experiment, he divided patients scheduled for removal of their gallbladder into two groups. For one group, Beecher paid a cursory visit on the night prior to surgery. He introduced himself and told the patients that he would see them in the morning. For the other group, Beecher's routine was totally different. He outlined in painstaking detail what would happen to them the next day: At 7:00 A.M. you will be given some medication by needle. The purpose of this medication is so and so. Then at 7:30, an orderly will come to your room and take you by stretcher to the preoperative room. There a nurse will start an intravenous drip. And so on, step by step, until the moment of return to the hospital room. Throughout the narrative, Beecher stopped for questions and made sure that the patient understood what he was saying.

The results were astounding. The carefully prepared group had fewer postoperative complications, a shorter length of stay in the hospital, required less postoperative attention, and consumed less pain medication. In short, this group handled surgery much better emotionally and medically than the control group. Their healing was enhanced. But why?

Mood and emotion are whole-body phenomena that alter the body's physiology and chemistry, as well as how that person feels and acts. Surgery is for most people a necessary but uncertain adventure. Uncertainty triggers anxiety or fear, which has physiological and psychological consequences. Beecher's careful preparation of his patients apparently lessened the patients' anxiety and thereby positively affected their healing. Patients knew what to expect; there were no surprises. In a lessened state of anxiety, confidence and trust soared, and healing was enhanced.

A Doula's Influence

Another study involving a doula showed how a patient's mood can influence health outcomes. A doula is a woman who has borne a child and is trained to attend to women in labor, usually a first labor. A doula is not a midwife or a nurse. The doula is a go-between between the patient and the hospital staff. In addition, a doula cares for the expectant mother's moment-by-moment needs for comfort—puffing up the pillow, holding her hand, playing soft music during contractions, or getting her a drink. The doula answers the mother's "What's next?" questions. Like Dr. Beecher, she offers comfort, allays anxiety, reduces isolation, and replaces uncertainty with experience-based facts.

The results of doula-attended births when compared with regular births were remarkable: There were fewer maternal and fetal complications, hospital stays were shorter, and Cesarean section rates were significantly decreased. Overall maternal satisfaction with the program was high. How does a doula's presence impact these obstetric outcomes? Apparently, the doula profoundly influences the mother's mood—she is less anxious, less uncertain, and more trusting. In short, the mother's body is in better condition to deliver the child.

These studies, along with many others and my experience with Reynell, continued to augment my medical training. New questions arose for me: What body functions are driven by my patients' moods? What are their automatic moods and emotions? And how do moods affect their bodily functions and their health?

A Matter of the Heart

That the heart is intimately tied to emotional life is evident in everyday experience. When you rush toward a friend or loved one in anticipation of reunion, your heart beats eagerly, as the poets say. When you're afraid or startled, your heart pounds. But does this have medical consequences?

In the 1950s, Dr. Meyer Friedman and Dr. Ray Rosenman, two cardiologists at the Mt. Zion Hospital in San Francisco, found that people who had a certain definable pattern of everyday behavior were more prone to heart attacks than people who did not have this pattern. They named these two patterns Type A and Type B.

A Type A person is prone to heart attack. Usually male, a Type A person is driven, always reaching for the next goal, rarely satisfied, difficult for others to keep up with, critical of himself and others, and often irritable. People may admire a Type A for his energy and drive, but they don't like to work closely with him—he's too unpredictable and demanding of himself and others. He's impossible to please.

A Type B person may be just as ambitious, but seeks his goals differently. He's team-oriented, capable of great effort, but also able to celebrate, give thanks, and have time for family and friends and renewal. Satisfaction, gratitude, and humility are present in this kind of person. A balanced life is his ideal.

We all know Type A's and B's. They exist in all walks of life, from bus drivers to rocket scientists. Type A and B styles are not styles of the mind, but habits of the whole body. They profoundly affect health. A Type A person generates metabolic and anatomical changes that lead to heart attacks, while Type B's have fewer heart attacks. Friedman and Rosenman's work suggested that mood affected longevity.

Redford Williams, a professor of medicine at Duke University, has built upon Friedman and Rosenman's work. Williams has devoted most of his professional life to deepening our understanding of the unity of emotional and physiological matters. His studies have to do with the relationship between anger and heart disease.

Angry people, he found, tend to react to adversity with a belligerent response that often includes blame, fault-finding, defensiveness, aggression, etc. This anger may be directed toward the self or toward others. For angry people this tendency is habitual, recurrent, and happens without thinking—it's automatic. He also discovered that such people suffered more than the expected frequency of heart attacks. Anger is a major cardiac risk factor.

Williams's work showed how the habitual response of a person is manifest not just in the psyche, but in his whole body. But that's not the end of it. The anger response influences a person's behavior, decisions, child-rearing, and personal habits. Angry people smoke and use alcohol and other substances more than other people. They tend to have belligerent social views, are often subject to impulsive if not criminal behavior, and they are not the kind of person we seek out when we have a problem.

This information violates the Cartesian notion of separate mind and body. Here a supposed mental state shows up in bodily changes and social and family behavior. Is anger a state of mind, a state of body, or a social matter? Obviously, it's all of these simultaneously. It's the manifestation of a whole person.

Walter, the Angry Man

Remember that Walter has had two heart attacks. By now, he was beginning to observe his anger, at least some of the time. When he listened to the information about anger and heart disease, Walter grew serious and quiet for a moment. Then he said, "That's me." But then anger took over once again and he shouted, "People can't change! That's the way I am!" in a belligerent tone of voice.

Moods, Emotions, and the Body

Your mood affects your whole body, including every cell.

The immune system is your elaborate system of defense against foreign invasion from outside substances and also from abnormal cells within your body. The system is composed of cells and their protein products called antibodies. Suppression of the system allows unwanted bacteria, viruses, and abnormal cancer precursor cells to grow. In short, suppression of your immune system can cause ill health.

In recent years, a number of scientific studies have shown this effect. David McClelland, the late Harvard psychologist, extensively studied the association of psychological state and immune function. In one of his most startling experiments, he measured IgA (an immune protein) in the blood and saliva of people after they viewed a horrifying movie about Hitler's atrocities, and then later after they saw an inspiring movie about Mother Teresa. The Mother Teresa movie enhanced IgA levels, the Hitler movie supressed them. People responded positively to Mother Teresa regardless of their religious persuasion. Viewing her unconditional love altered the people's bodies and their immune defenses!

In another study, Janice Kiecolt-Glaser and her husband, Ronald Glaser, two investigators from Ohio State University, examined the effects of marital disruption on the immune system. They found that women who had been separated one year or less had significant suppression of their cellular immune function. Perhaps as a consequence, separated and divorced patients have a greater than average incidence of illness and are more than six times more likely to be admitted to a hospital than married people. Obviously, divorce can change the mood and the body and perhaps make it more vulnerable to illness.

Of course, the immune system is not the only system involved in emotional expression. The musculoskeletal system is involved in mood. We can see mood and emotion on the face and in the body of another person. Depressed people look sad. Anxious people look frightened.

Also, the cardiovascular and circulatory systems are deeply influenced by emotions and moods, as we've shown. A group of Finnish investigators recently published a study that further supports this idea. They subjected a group of men to a mental stress test. They then checked the men's blood pressure as a way to measure vascular reactivity. The results? Some men when stressed reacted with extreme blood pressure elevations. Alarmingly, those men had permanent narrowing of the blood vessels that feed the brain. They were much more at risk of having a stroke. The scientists concluded that these men seem to be Type A personalities, those driven to be perfect. Again, a powerful connection between mental and physiological processes—stress and contraction of arteries.

A powerful theme emerges from these and many other research studies: Your moods and emotions are not isolated psychological events; they involve your entire body. Your health and wellness are functions of your emotional life and your skills for living as well as your linguistic behavior, as we have suggested in chapter 4.

Moods and Emotions Are
Structurally Determined

How did you get to have the moods and emotions that you have? Why are some people fearful, some aggressive and angry, some depressed, and some chronically anxious? And even more important, is there anything you can do about it?

Robert, the High Achiever

Robert observed that his life was a "setup" for his anxiety and misery. He felt he was destined to be a great lawyer, but he didn't know why he wanted to be a lawyer. As he talked in class, he began to realize that his parents had planted this profession in his mind. Not only that, but they had insisted that Robert had to be the best lawyer in Boston. "What pressure!" he said. "No wonder I'm always worried."

Remember our earlier discussion about structural determinism? Moods and emotions live in your structure, waiting to be triggered by life's events. One person when asked to do mental arithmetic may become invigorated and moved to higher acuity; another may become fearful of error; a third may become angry. They are all acting in ways determined by their structural state, their inherited equipment modified by their history.

So how did their emotional structure get that way? First, just as you inherited certain physical equipment, you also inherited certain emotional responses. For example, depression tends to run in families, especially kinds such as manic depression. The same is true of other emotions. The Harvard researcher Jerome Kagan has shown that certain infants have the character trait of shyness from birth.

But in addition to what you inherit, your structure is altered by your experiences of living. You develop certain automatic understandings of life. And your body is emotionally in perfect harmony and consistency with this knowledge. For example, children of upwardly mobile parents tend to be aggressive, seeing life as a challenge to be mastered or overcome. Children of alcoholics, on the other hand, may be highly distrustful. When they must rely on others, they may become vigilant and anxious, eventually falling ill.

Linda, the Perfectionist

Linda said, "I live in a world in which I feel I'm stupid and hopeless. I have adopted as my view of life the story others tell about me. No wonder I'm depressed. It's useful to see this, but can I change?"

"Only if you stay awake," I said. "If you don't understand me now, you will later on."

Like other actions, our emotions are structurally determined, recurrent, and happen before reflection. I experienced this effect myself when I began to do a lot of public speaking.

Stage Fright

About the time I was learning about moods and emotions, I received a number of requests to lecture publically about my clinic at the Harvard Community Health Plan. But there was a big problem—I was terrified of public speaking. The night before I was to give my initial speech at a local hospital, I meticulously wrote out my presentation. Even as I wrote, my body became anxious. I was afraid that I wouldn't be able to read the speech. I kept jumping up from the chair and getting a drink and food to quiet myself.

The next day at the clinic I shuddered each time I thought of the evening's presentation. This same dread accompanied me on the ride to the hospital and as I entered the auditorium. As I walked in, I noticed that the auditorium was packed with doctors, nurses, and even patients. "Oh, no!" I thought. As the moderator, a pleasant-faced young woman named Julie, approached me, I felt like fleeing out the door. "Dr. Budd, it's so good to see you," she gushed. "Everyone is looking forward to your speech." Everyone but me.

Finally, the time came. As Julie introduced me, my palms were sweating and my heart was pounding. I couldn't even hear what she was saying. I took the podium and proceeded to read my talk, hardly ever making eye contact with the audience. When I did, my glances were automatic and inauthentic as I struggled not to appear nervous. My talk was lifeless. The audience was polite, but I was disappointed. I had delivered my message from a frightened body, and hence was not convincing.

Lecture requests continued to come in, however. Each time as I took the podium, my body repeated the same routine that it had done for years, ever since high school. And each time my message was blunted. I was frustrated. I even considered using a drug called a beta-blocker, which inhibits the stress response.

In desperation I went to a hypnotist named Lou, who is known for his ability to deal with phobias, especially fear of flying. During my first session, as Lou began to induce deep relaxation in me by suggestion, I remember thinking, "This is all hocus-pocus." When I was fully relaxed, with my eyes closed, Lou said, "Imagine yourself in front of an audience beginning to speak. Let yourself see that clearly and feel a little bit of what you generally feel. When you feel the sensations, raise your hand."

I recall imagining the hospital audience and as I did, I could feel my heart beginning to pound. I raised my hand. After a few seconds, Lou told me to breathe deeply and let go of the tension. He had me do this over and over, session after session, for longer periods of time. During every session I would experience my reaction to fear for a longer and longer time. I got used to it, instead of running from it. I gradually began to let myself have all of the sensation. As I did, it seemed to lighten a bit.

After a while Lou told me his secret: "You'll overcome this reaction by letting yourself have it fully, not by running away from it. If you do, it will chase you." Only after several sessions did this paradox seem a remote possibility.

Because of this new insight, I decided to change my lecture itself. I would begin with a detailed description of the stress response. I packed in all the details I could think of—what was going on with my hormones, their impact on my mouth, my hands, my heart, my thinking, etc. And each time, as I described these sensations, I let myself feel them. I shared my feelings with the audience to illustrate the normal stress response.

After a while, something miraculous happened. Each time that I spoke, there was less and less to describe. My embodied response was changing. Today, I have only the slightest twinge of fear before I speak, just enough to mobilize my thinking and alertness.

This experience taught me something very important about change and learning on an emotional level. Like Lou said, you must go *into* your automatic emotions rather than flee from them. This was counterintuitive logically but true to my experience and that of my teachers and many of my patients.

A Conversation with Morrie

One of the most eloquent of my teachers is Morrie Schwartz. Although I never met him, I learned from him through a wonderful book about his life called *Tuesdays with Morrie*. Morrie was a professor of sociology at Brandeis University, a skillful teacher well loved by his students, fellow faculty members, and friends. He was both learned and wise, a rare combination. In his old age, Morrie became ill with Lou Gehrig's disease and was forced to stay at home. A former student, sports reporter Mitch Albom, visited Morrie every Tuesday. Albom recorded their conversations, and they form the content of his book.

One conversation with Morrie is particularly appropriate as you think about altering your emotions and moods. One day, Albom asked Morrie how he was approaching death. Morrie said, "What I am doing is detaching myself. This is important for someone like me who is dying, but is more important for someone like you who is perfectly healthy."

Albom was puzzled by this statement because Morrie had always preached involvement in, not detachment from, life. When he expressed his confusion, Morrie responded with the following statement:

> Detachment does not mean that you don't let the experience penetrate you. [Recall how Lou had me experience my fear fully.] On the contrary, you let it penetrate you to your core. That's how you are able to leave it. Take any emotion . . . like what I'm going through, fear and pain from a deadly illness. If you hold back on the emotions you can never get to being detached. You are too busy being afraid. But by throwing yourself into these emotions, by allowing yourself to dive in, over your head even, you experience them fully and completely. You know what love is, you know what pain is, you know what grief is. Then you can say, "All right. Now I have experienced that emotion, now I need to detach from it for a moment." I know you think this is just about dying. But I keep telling you, when you learn how to die, you learn how to live.

Morrie soon died peacefully. His wisdom is not self-evident in our technological culture in which taking pain away is the goal. But some of life's pains, its emotional ups and downs, are unavoidable. The wisdom that Morrie lived—embracing the emotion, knowing the emotion in all of its dimensions—takes courage. But it is the only way to learn how to alter your moods and emotions and significantly affect your body's structure.

EXERCISES

Major Points in Chapter 5

□ Moods and emotions are always in the background of your life, giving it color and texture.

□ People tend to be poor observers of their moods and the moods of others. Because of this, your ability to use your moods constructively, which has come to be called emotional intelligence, is probably not great.

□ Moods can be seen as embodied assessments of the future or of the past, or judgments about future safety and success.

□ People have moods, families and cities have moods, companies have moods. Moods determine what is and is not possible.

□ Moods and emotions are structurally determined and learned. Generally, you don't think about what mood you want to be in, you "fall into it."

□ Moods and emotions are whole-body phenomena, neither exclusively mental nor physical, but both simultaneously. Moods and emotions defy the Cartesian view of the world.

□ Moods and emotions profoundly influence your health. This fact is well documented for heart disease. Moods can also significantly alter your immune system.

A Brief Check on Previous Learning

In chapter 1, you began to examine yourself as a learner. How are you doing with completing the exercises and meditating? Do you see old barriers to learning possessing you? If you do, face them and go *into* them. By now you should be meditating five time a week for at least ten to twenty minutes each time.

Use the awareness exercise to sharpen your observation of your moods. When you sit down to meditate, note what mood you're in. As different thoughts automatically arise, see if your mood changes and what thoughts you have then. Become aware of the unity of thinking, speaking, and moods.

In chapter 2, you began to observe your body as a structurally determined system. Are you listening to your body as it's triggered in the course of a day? Are you observing the bodies of others at work, home, socially, etc.?

In chapter 3, we examined the role of history in shaping who you are, what you see, how you react, and what you do. By this time, you should be having insights into your history's impact on shaping who you are at this very moment.

Finally, in chapter 4, you started to make distinctions in the domain of language. How are your observations of your languaging habits coming along? Are you requesting more clearly and declining when appropriate? Are you listening to assessments as assessments? Can you begin to see the connection between your linguistic behavior and your mood?

Exercises for Reflection and Learning

Moods and Emotions—Exercise One: Moods as Embodied Assessments

I've claimed that moods can be seen as embodied assessments. The two functions of the body, languaging and feeling, are deeply connected. In this exercise you'll experience the connection.

□ Go into a room and close the door. Sit in a chair, alertly but comfortably.

□ Follow the instructions for each of the four exercises.

□ When doing each exercise, notice what happens to your body. What mood does it fall into? Is this a familiar or a foreign mood to you?

□ After a minute or two, stand up, stretch, take some deep breaths, walk around a bit, and recenter yourself. When you're ready, sit back down in your chair and repeat the process for the next exercise.

FIRST ASSESSMENT

I have too much to do. My to-do list is huge. I can work hard and fast but I still won't finish. I end the day half done. I'm overwhelmed. Even if I go faster and faster and faster, I never do it all. There are serious negative consequences if I don't finish. But there is just too much to do.

Read this statement three times. The first time read it silently. Then say it out loud two more times, faster and louder with each utterance. Put spirit and passion into these readings, as if you're auditioning for a role in a movie.

Now close your eyes and observe your body. What changes have occurred in your muscles, your breathing, your circulation? Has your posture changed? What emotion or mood are you in? What does the world look like to someone in this mood? In this mood or emotion what actions are possible? What ones are difficult or impossible? How often are you in this mood? Most people would call this mood anxiety. Take notes.

Gretchen found this exercise very powerful. It helped her to see a connection between her embodied narratives and moods—her anxiety.

Notes on the First Assessment

SECOND ASSESSMENT

You've hurt me! Your actions have caused me harm, which I didn't deserve. You should have known better, you didn't meet my expectations. You are cruel. I'm very angry with you. Somewhere, sometime, somehow, I'll get even. People like you just can't be trusted. You are scary.

Read this statement three times. Read it silently the first time. Then say it out loud two more times, louder and with more emotion each time. Again, put spirit and passion into this reading.

After this, close your eyes and observe your body. What emotion or mood are you in? What does the world look like to someone in this mood? In this mood or emotion what actions are possible or impossible? Is this mood or emotion the same or different from those triggered by the first assessment? Is this emotion common for you? Most people would call this mood anger.

After he read this statement, Walter said he felt this way most of the time. Even doing the exercise he became angry.

Notes on the Second Assessment

THIRD ASSESSMENT

The future is hopeless. Nothing is going right or will ever change. There is nothing I or anyone else can do. Even God can't help. Things will never get better. I'll always feel as I do now—terrible.

Read this statement three times. Read it silently the first time. Then say it out loud two times, in a slow, lethargic way.

After this, close your eyes and observe your body. What emotion or mood are you in? What does the world look like to someone in this mood? In this mood or emotion what actions are possible, what ones difficult or impossible? Is this mood or emotion the same or different from those triggered by the first two assessments? Is this mood common for you? Most people would call this mood depression.

Linda said that this assessment described her perfectly and that she often felt this way.

Notes on the Third Assessment

FOURTH ASSESSMENT

I'm flawed and insufficient. No matter how hard I try, I'll never succeed. I'll be found out by others; they know how bad I am. If I take risks, my imperfections will be discovered. So I'll be cautious and quiet. Maybe nobody will notice me.

Read this three times. Read it silently the first time. Then say it out loud two times, in a subdued, withdrawn tone.

After this, close your eyes and observe your body. What emotion or mood are you in? What does the world look like to someone in this mood? In this mood or emotion what actions are possible, what ones difficult or impossible? Is this mood or emotion the same or different from that triggered by the first three assessments? Do you ever fall into this mood? Most people call it low self-esteem or a mood of embarrassment.

Robert said that this statement helped him understand that underneath all of his striving for success in life was a sense that he was unworthy. He realized that his achievements were a way of hiding these feelings.

Notes on the Fourth Assessment

These exercises can help show you the deep connections between mood, emotion, and language. People often live as if they were making continual ungrounded assessments about themselves, others, and their future. Despite this, these assessments produce real changes in their bodies. Recognizing this reality can give you the motivation to take new actions. If you can notice these old assessments in your body, and can feel them deeply, you'll free yourself of their mysterious hold on your life. Once you see them, you can ask yourself how valid these assessments are. Do I have to do everything? Are others really out to get me? Is the future totally hopeless? Am I deeply flawed as a person?

In these exercises you've examined the relationship between languaging and emotions and have generated some different moods and emotions in your body. Which ones of the above seem foreign to you, and which ones were familiar to you? Take notes on this question and any other observations you've made.

Notes
(Moods and Emotions—Exercise One)

Moods and Emotions—Exercise Two: the Walking-Down-the-Street Exercise

You had an exercise similar to this one in chapter 2's exercise section called Observing the Bodies of Others. This exercise goes deeper into the influence of mood and emotion on your body, on your perception, on how you feel, and on what you do. Do this exercise respectfully so that people don't feel that you're making fun of them.

Walk down a crowded street. Notice someone. Give a name to the mood that he or she is in: happy, anxious, depressed, flirtatious, angry, pressured, etc. After you pass by this person, put your body into that mood. Mimic the facial expression, the gait, the breathing, and the posture of that person. Walk along in that body for a few moments.

What does the world look like in that body? Does it look safe, nurturing, supportive, or dangerous in some way? What thoughts come up automatically in this body? What assessments of yourself and your future do you have in this body? What actions could not take place in this body? What does it feel like to have that body? Are you ever in this mood? Is it familiar or foreign to you?

Do this for several different people.

In the space provided, make notes on the following questions:

☐ How was this exercise for you now compared to when you did the earlier exercise?

☐ Can you see that you have new distinctions for seeing?

☐ Who in your life embodies the moods that have been captured by this exercise? Do you have more compassion for them now?

Notes
(Moods and Emotions—Exercise Two)

Moods and Emotions—Exercise Three: the Music Exercise

This exercise is a variation of exercise 3 in chapter 2's exercise section. It's best done with a push-button radio like a car radio, but any radio will do.

Put the radio on at a comfortable volume. You should be relaxed and seated. If you use your car radio, make sure the car is parked.

Switch to a music station and listen to the music. Let your body relax and move with the music.

☐ What mood does this music put you into?
☐ What does this mood feel like in your body?
☐ Can you begin to see why you like certain kinds of music and not others?

Do this for at least four additional stations. Pick different styles such as popular, classical, country, rock, rap, etc.

In the space provided, make notes on the following questions:

☐ First, how was this exercise for you now compared to when you did the earlier exercise? Can you see that you have new distinctions and that you have learned something?

☐ Second, whom do you know who embodies the moods captured by this exercise?

☐ Finally, what can you learn about a culture or nationality by its music? Can you see how different music goes with different cultural groups?

Respect is living with the music of another without judgment.

Notes
(Moods and Emotions—Exercise Three)

Music, along with colors, foods, making and receiving assessments, and declining requests all have the power to shift your mood. The first step in using your moods constructively is to observe them. That's what we've begun to do in these exercises.

The Experiences of My Patients in Doing These Exercises

Gretchen, the Perfectionist

When she did the first assessment, Gretchen's old feelings came back. She felt anxious and her stomach rumbled. She was amazed that the simple affirmation represented in that statement actually bothered her stomach.

"I have to do something about this, starting now. Doctors can't help me with this," Gretchen said. She declared herself a beginner in learning to live her own life, not a life driven by the fundamentalist "rights and wrongs" of her past.

Walter, the Angry Man

Walter resonated with the second assessment. He described the familiarity he felt as his muscles and face tensed in anger. Walter said that he spent at least half of each day in this mood. When I asked him what, from his point of view, this had to do with his heart condition, he replied, "Everything! I'm sure of it."

In the Walking-Down-the-Street exercise, Walter came upon someone who reminded him of himself. His first reaction to this person was one of compassion, not his usual reaction of cynicism. Instead, Walter thought, "That poor sucker is going to end up like me."

I suggested that he was beginning to show compassion for himself. Walter smiled and nodded.

Linda, the Depressed Woman

Linda responded deeply to the third and fourth assessments. Her lifelong feelings of hopelessness and embarrassment had sapped her dignity, her vitality, and her ambition. Now, for the first time, Linda began to see that these past assessments were ungrounded. She felt tremendous sadness at a life lived under a false spell. At the same time, she began to show elation at the possibility of a different future.

I explained to her that we all live under one spell or another, but that learning and change were possible, within limits. I told her that her choice seemed to be between a life of certain despair and one of possible change. Linda said that for the first time she felt she could change.

Robert, the High Achiever

Robert's response surprised me. I thought that he would recognize anxiety as his pervasive mood. Instead, he said that the fourth mood, embarrassment or a feeling of deep insufficiency, was the one that "hooked" him.

"For me, life looks like achieve or perish," he said. He realized that others defined what achievement meant. "I'll never be at peace!" Robert cried. I replied that as long as his idea of insufficiency went unexamined and ungrounded, that would be his reality.

Putting It All Together

Autobiography in Five Chapters

1. I walk down the street.
   There is a huge hole in the sidewalk.
   I fall in.
   I'm lost . . . hopeless.
   It's not my fault.
   It takes forever to get out.

2. I walk down the same street.
   There is a huge hole in the sidewalk.
   I pretend that I don't see it.
   I fall in again.
   I can't believe that I am in the same place again.
   But it's not my fault.
   Still, it takes me a long time to get out.

3. I walk down the same street.
   There is a huge hole in the sidewalk.
   I see it.
   Still I fall in. It's a habit.
   My eyes are wide open.
   Already I know where I am.
   It's my fault.
   I climb out quickly.

4. I walk down the same street.
   There is a huge hole in the sidewalk.
   I walk around it.

5. I walk down a different street.
                                    —Portia Nelson

The true value of a human being is determined primarily by the measure and sense in which he has attained liberation from the self.

— ALBERT EINSTEIN

Awareness of the environment is a property of cognition at all levels of life. Awareness of self is manifest only in higher animals and fully unfolds in the human mind.

— FRITJOF CAPRA

I n the first five chapters of this book, I've discussed some of the major ideas I've learned over the past twenty years regarding a new approach to health. You've shared with me my journey of understanding. In this chapter, I want to show you how these ideas can be woven into a tapestry of understanding and wellness—a whole both useful and grounded.

But before I do, I want to introduce you to David Bohm, who has articulated in an elegant way this book's message and helped me understand how to create a new mind. When I first read his work, I marveled at his clarity. Here is what he said.

Thought as a System

In 1994, David Bohm, a Nobel Prize–winning British quantum physicist at the University of London, published *Thought as a System,* a book inspired by his lifelong work in physics, but whose focus was human life. In the book, Bohm showed how a person's "system of thought" affected his or her life:

The tacit assumption in thought is that it's just telling you the way things are and that it is not doing anything. Thought, however, gives the false information that you are running it, that you are the one who controls thought, whereas actually *thought is the one that controls each one of us* [my italics]. Until thought is understood—better yet, more than understood, perceived—it will actually control us.

Bohm's statement underscores much of what I've been discussing. First, that thought shows you a world. When you're depressed, the world looks hopeless; if you're anxious, the world looks demanding and frightening; when you're angry, the world looks hostile and unsupportive. Second, thought fools you into thinking that it reflects the world as it is. Because of this, you may relinquish responsibility and control of your life. And third, until you perceive your thought in action, it controls your life. Thought hides itself.

Bohm also recognized the connectivity of thought and its presence in all body functions. The body is one piece, each part connected with all others by nerves, peptides, hormones, etc., so that it acts as a single unity. In Bohm's words:

> The system not only includes thought and feelings, but it includes the state of the body, its actions; it includes the whole of society as thought is passing back and forth between people in a process by which thought evolved from ancient times.

As you read these lines, recall the lecture I described to you in chapter 4 where Fernando Flores had participants repeat an affirmation of depression. The participants universally reported that their bodies felt depressed after they made the affirmation.

If thought is structurally determined and shows you a world, and at the same time hides itself while it's doing its work, what happens to our freedom? Are we all merely captives of our very own system? Can we learn and change? Or are we destined to repeat and repeat our habits, good and bad, to the end?

Bohm has addressed these questions in his book, using the analogy of physical movement. We can catch the system at work in the physical domain. People, he reminds us, have internal mechanisms that "observe" and coordinate their physical movements. We coordinate millions of innate reflexes into physical movements, which produce a golf swing, the playing of a Chopin nocturne, or the driving of a car. In fact, we do this without thinking.

When you learn a new physical activity like tennis, you have to pay attention actively and learn each movement carefully. Later, such adjustments happen unconsciously, without thinking. Different body mechanisms govern the proper coordination of feet, muscles, bones, etc. It's as if there's an internal observer and coordinator built into your structure that is activated without thinking.

Such physical awareness is called *proprioception*. Bohm suggested that:

Proprioception should be extended into the area of thought so that we are aware of thought as it participates. What you think affects what you perceive outside and how you feel inside.

With such awareness, possibility for adjustment arises, as in muscular movement. Thought's grip on you lessens. You can feel this in your own body. People sometimes refer to this as an "aha" experience. The philosopher Martin Heidegger used the term "releasment" to describe this awareness-driven freedom.

Now you may begin to understand why we've been building distinctions for you to observe your somatic, linguistic, and emotional behavior as it happens in life. We've been attempting, in the preceding chapters, to give you tools to shed light on phenomena that have been going on all of the time, but without your awareness. Now you can begin to witness these processes. And in the very act of attentive witnessing, you can be released from the grip of their automaticity.

This process—the mechanism that allows us to witness thought—thus far escapes description scientifically. The problem, obviously, is how to become aware of something that "hides its true nature," as thought does.

The purpose of the exercise sections, particularly the awareness exercises, is to have you begin the process of witnessing in your own life using the distinctions of this book. You will seriously engage, if you choose to do so, in building "proprioception" of your own system of thought, of being.

In the introduction to the exercise sections, I discussed some of the issues involved in achieving this goal. Chief among them is finding the courage to tell and accept the truth. At that moment, your stories of blame and victimization about why you suffer fall away. But at the same moment, the possibilities for creating a new mind and body emerge. That was the case with my mother. A moment came in her life at a crucial time when she saw and told the truth, and this act gave her life. It always does.

My Mother at Ninety-two

My mother, Lillian, is ninety-two and a proud woman like her mother, Minnie. At an early age she showed an affinity and aptitude for music. With Minnie's support, she became an accomplished pianist. She owned a grand piano at age fifteen, the fruits of Minnie's hard labor.

Lillian married Mark, my father, in her twenties. They were both performing musicians and suffered during the Great Depression because of a lack of work. To make ends meet, they gave music lessons to children. As the Depression abated, they started a children's summer camp for their music students. My mother and father's timing was perfect. They opened their camp at the moment when business began to improve and families again had resources to spend on their children.

For almost forty years thereafter they operated a superb camp, a place of joy and learning. They felt great pride in this accomplishment.

Lillian and Mark were independent and ran things at the camp in a certain way—with an iron hand in a velvet glove. Each summer they were responsible for more than a hundred children and a large staff. My mother and father approached this responsibility with diligence and control, building strong habits of being in charge. They planned the meals, designed the musical activities, hired and supervised the staff, etc. All of the comings and goings of this summer community were under their thumbs.

After my father's death, Lillian, then age eighty-five, came to live with my family. It was not easy either for her or for us. My mother's independence and habits of managing others often clashed with our family's needs and values—but we made do.

When she turned ninety-one, her age began to take its toll. She had difficulty climbing stairs, she was afraid to be alone, and she became alarmed by any physical symptom, fearing that it was a precursor to illness. Given her habits of a lifetime, my mother struggled to keep control rather than to accept the help she needed. But the tides of time roll on. After a while, my sister and I, with the reluctant consent of my mother, decided that a nearby assisted living facility would be the best place for her. We made the proper arrangements for the move.

As Bohm said, people function as an integrated system of thoughts, feelings, bodily responses, actions, etc. My mother's system was one of being independent and in charge of her environment and the people in it. With the change in living arrangements, she found herself in a situation that most people would call charming, comfortable, safe, and caring. But she was very unhappy.

Instead of being relieved at having the burdens of daily living lifted from her shoulders, my mother was miserable. For her, conditioned and shaped as she was to be in charge, the facility was filled with problems: the apartment wasn't of her design or choice; she had to interact with people that she didn't know or choose to be with; she had to eat food that she neither selected nor prepared. She had lost control of her life. Her used-to-being-in-control body clashed with her present reality. She suffered.

How was this structural discord manifested? How did this underlying "system of thought" reveal itself? The first manifestation was criticism and complaint. My mother lashed out at the managers of the facility, calling them "dictators," and she ridiculed the employees. One morning when I was visiting her she said, "This place is like being in a concentration camp."

Her suffering also manifested itself in her mood. She became depressed. As she did, she began to forget things to such a degree that she was sometimes disoriented. My mother, a virtuoso since her youth, lost interest in her lifelong passion for music—she stopped listening to her weekly opera and symphony broadcasts. Her piano was silent.

When her friends offered to visit her, she declined.

Simultaneously, her heart condition, which had been under control, became worse. She developed congestive heart failure. Her physicians couldn't understand her rapid deterioration—they could detect no new damage of her heart. Each new medication seemed to produce unwanted side effects such as rashes or nausea.

My mother's system of thought—a system of independence, pride, and control—was brutally challenged by the change to the assisted living home. Her way of living, her moods, her emotions, her physiology, her health—all were in disarray. *Who* she was and *where* she was in life and in residence clashed savagely. The price of this conflict was being paid in loss of health and wellness. She saw no possibility for existence in this environment. Her body reflected her hopelessness—it was giving up.

Growing Old with Peace and Dignity

My family began to consider moving her out of the facility. But before we did, two things happened. First, we hired a physical therapist to massage my mother's tense muscles and teach her relaxation techniques.

From what you now know, you can see that we were attempting to shift her body from tense and resistant to relaxed and flexible. Since I had come to see the body as a system of connected functions, my hope was that in so doing, her thoughts too would soften.

Initially my mother resisted these sessions saying, "What good will they do? I hate this place." Despite this resistance, as the therapist worked with her and her muscles relaxed, her mood also lightened. At one point she said to me, "When my body is calm, my life looks better." But gains were temporary and seemed to wane between sessions. As each session with the therapist slipped into the distance, her "system of thought" seized her again and she fell into hopelessness.

Simultaneously, a second thing happened. After hearing of my work with the Ways to Wellness program, the director of my mother's facility invited me to conduct a weekly workshop on the issues of aging, death, and living with assistance. I agreed and called the course "Growing Old with Peace and Dignity."

As I began the program, I quickly realized that most of the residents shared my mother's pain of giving up control, although none with her intensity. Some more clearly acknowledged the change as a necessity. Others were actually grateful for the help offered to them as their abilities waned. My mother, who attended the course, at first listened to the other residents with contempt. She told me, "They must be weak people to accept this like sheep." Gradually, however, she became more tolerant of her fellow residents' attitudes and curious about how they could accept this way of living.

Somewhere in the middle of the ten-session course, I asked the class two questions: "How do you want to live each day?" and "How do you want to die?" For most people, these are shocking and personal questions, but our class had developed a certain honesty and trust, and the participants engaged with me. I told the class that I raised this question because I had read *Tuesdays with Morrie,* the book I referred to earlier. In the book, the author Mitch Albom asks Morrie, "How can you ever be prepared to die?" Morrie replied, "Do what the Buddhists do. Every day, have a little bird on your shoulder that asks, 'Is today the day? Am I ready? Am I doing all I need to do? Am I being the person I want to be?' "

This passage and my questions opened emotional floodgates for the residents. Passion in the form of tears flowed. People spoke of the unspeakable—death. They told their "truths" about being old—their innermost fears, their disappointments, their losses, and their considerable accomplishments. Among the course members were writers, actors, professors, parents, and even a prizefighter.

Before this session, people didn't even know about others' backgrounds. They were "faceless residents." But at this moment of "truthfulness," the residents began to observe their deepest thoughts, to share their concerns, and, in our terms, to acknowledge the movement of their system of thought and to speak of that system with accepting awareness.

Complaining and grumbling melted away. The glow of their common humanity shone through.

Then, to my amazement, my mother, who rarely shares herself in public, spoke about how difficult it was for her to live at the facility and not "control" her life. As I listened to her make this observation, I noticed that her body relaxed and tears rolled down her cheeks. As her "system of thought" was revealed to her own awareness, and in public, its grip lessened. The phrase "The truth will set you free" played through my head.

The session went on. Dan, an eighty-seven-year-old former writer, complained about his nightly serving of tepid soup. Other residents chimed in that they hated the soup they were being served. But Dan's mood was no longer one of complaint and resignation. He asked for ideas about how to change this situation. One resident replied, "Let's form a food committee to convey our requests for better food to the director." Another resident turned to my mother and said, "Lillian, you know how to prepare food for large numbers of people because of your camp experience. Would you be our chairwoman?" When a number of other residents also urged my mother to take the job, she accepted.

After this session, life slowly improved for my mother. She began to see her habits and was not as deeply immersed in them. She began to complain less and act more. Her mood gradually lightened somewhat, although she still had ups and downs. At the same time, her physical condition improved and her heart problems lessened. She had a breakthrough.

She also began to develop friendships with some of the residents. Her opinion of the management changed from feeling that they were a band of captors to recognizing some who were helpers. She introduced me to a new head of recreation saying, "She is a wonderful person."

My mother soon realized that there were areas of her life she could still control—when to wake up and when go to sleep, what to read, whether to go to a movie, when to eat, whether or not to play a game of bridge, etc. She made friends with a woman named Barbara, who had an enthusiastic and creative attitude toward life, and with Kurt, a former college professor.

My mother had some limited triumphs as the food committee chairwoman. The dining room now served hot soup. And she arranged to have several of her recipes, handed down from Minnie, on the menu. Her fellow residents lauded her for her efforts.

This past spring, one of my mother's friends reached her one hundredth birthday. In celebration, my mother and her grandchild, Jessie, put on a concert. Jessie is a brilliant young singer, and my mother accompanied her at the piano. Both were dressed in their concert finery as they filled the room with music. I glanced around and saw not a dry eye, except on stage. There my mother held her head high with dignity and pride.

Nothing had changed for her—the same aging, the same assisted living home, the same staff, etc.—but everything had changed as her system of thought lessened its grip.

Linda, the Depressed Woman

As I was telling my mother's story, Linda began to sob.

She said, "I'm so inspired by your mother. I've been living in hopelessness for years. Somewhere deep inside I know, and I've always known, that this was a lie. I am not stupid. There is a lot that I can do well, but the old attitude keeps coming up—like it did for your mother. I'm so confused, I don't know what to do now."

I acknowledged Linda's new insights and her courage at facing the truth and suggested she be patient and persistent.

The Three A's of Learning

In this section, I present to you a general structure for incorporating into your life the distinctions of this book. All of the learning, the new distinctions, the thinking that we have been doing together is useless unless we can live it. But how do we begin to weave a tapestry of learning?

After observing myself and thousands of patients, I can describe several stages in the process of learning and growth. On each person's individual path there are changes in tempo—breakthroughs, plateaus, accelerations, and regressions. But still we can distinguish three underlying themes that support growth. They can be conveniently summarized as *awareness, acceptance,* and *action,* what I call the Three A's of Learning. Let's take each separately.

Awareness

Awareness is our foundation of freedom and growth. Yet for most of us it is the central challenge of life to see that which by its very nature obscures itself—ourselves. Awareness therefore involves exquisite honesty, telling the truth, and making a commitment to see yourself as you really are, with all of your fears, anxieties, needs, greediness, jealousies, and strengths. Only when you view these learned tendencies in your life, and "experience them fully" as Bohm said, can you hope to move toward freedom—to wake up to the present moment.

Blame, denial, resentment, and victimization keep us stuck and motionless. My mother's explanations about how bad everyone and everything was exacted a heavy toll on her. With awareness and acknowledgment life energy showed itself again. So too for all of us. When we are able to see our habits and how they operate, new freedom and energy is available.

Of course, some circumstances are horrible and justify your anger and disdain. But even at our most horrible moments, we can learn about ourselves as observers.

This was true for Sidney Rittenberg, a young man in the U.S. Army during World War II with special training in the Chinese language. After the war, Rittenberg became the English translator for Chairman Mao. At the time of the Chinese Cultural Revolution, in 1968, Rittenberg was jailed for political reasons. He remained in jail for nine years, some of that time in solitary confinement.

Can you imagine the conversations of anger, longing, resentment, and despair that such a situation would trigger? For most of us, as was the case with the many others who were jailed with Rittenberg, we would suffer ourselves to death. Rittenberg somehow discovered a way to quiet his automatic negative conversations—he would take a deep breath and engage in an activity that required enormous concentration. For example, he cleaned his cell meticulously each day, polishing the bars and the walls. He read avidly and kept a diary. He wrote long, detailed letters that were never sent.

The prison guards noticed Rittenberg's efforts and realized he was "flourishing" in this horrible environment. They began to admire him. As a result, they brought him more books and increased his daily ration of food, as well as other comforts. With such help, Rittenberg survived the ordeal and was finally released.

For me, Rittenberg represents the power of living in the moment. He embraced this horrible time with self-awareness and became an observer of his habitual conversations that generate suffering. Circumstances may produce pain; people produce their own suffering. Rittenberg was not a "special" person; he was just like you or me. He survived through self-discipline of the deepest and most powerful kind.

Awareness involves experiencing every moment in all its fullness and aliveness, in contrast to living in your interpretation of it. For example, sometimes when I see my children, I find myself possessed by the thought that I wish I could see them more often. Even as they are in front of me, I am suffering because of an internal thought of insufficiency. This longing distracts me even while they're visiting me. Isn't that crazy? We all are like this unless we wake up.

Imagine experiencing each moment, the joyful and the painful ones, without blame, resentment, or attempting to escape by diversion. This is the power of awareness—of seeing how you keep yourself from the truth of the moment by your habits of seeing. To achieve awareness requires discipline, commitment, distinctions for seeing, and often a coach, teacher, or friend—a human mirror. In a "lone ranger" society where asking for help and conversation is seen as weakness, this is difficult. It's time to break through that and rebuild healing communities. In business, they call this a "learning organization." Let's become learning organizations.

This is the central discipline of our dojo—a disciplined commitment to telling the truth, waking up to the moment just as it is.

Easier said than done. Being a Buddha or a Christ is not the point. Entering onto the path *is* the point. Only lifelong practice creates such a state of being. The philosopher Søren Kierkegaard said:

> In order to swim one takes off all one's clothes; in order to aspire to the truth one must undress in a far more inward sense, divest oneself of all one's inward clothes, of thoughts, conceptions, selfishness, etc. before one is sufficiently naked.

Gretchen, the Perfectionist

Gretchen said, "I'm beginning to see that my body gets triggered fifty times each day because I'm a perfectionist. I wonder, 'Am I getting worse, or have I been this way all along?' I get triggered when I have to do something important or when I'm uncertain. I'm so afraid of not doing it 'right' or 'perfectly' that I tense up, and I make the mistakes I'm afraid of. Being a perfectionist is, in a way, the 'who' that I am. I feel sad, and want to laugh at the same time, when I realize what a good 'perfectionist' machine I've been."

I told Gretchen that this mixture of sadness and joy is often present at the moment of seeing that, as Jon Kabat-Zinn says, "wherever you go, there you are." I urged her to be patient and persistent.

MEDITATIVE TECHNIQUES

The awareness muscle is part of your structure, but most likely it needs considerable strengthening. Meditative techniques, developed in the East, are a physical and emotional practice that builds your awareness muscle.

I hope you have begun to meditate already. I urge regularity and diligence in the practice. For those who do not meditate, follow my instructions in the first chapter and commit yourself to trying. Daily meditation is like an "awareness gym" for life. It strengthens your ability to be here in the present, not elsewhere in worry.

Various other forms of prayer and solitude build awareness. During a walk in the woods, you can observe the thoughts that take you away from the sounds, sights, and smells of nature. Or, when you visit the seashore, you can become aware of what keeps you from being with the smells and sounds of the ocean. If you don't see these tendencies, they'll continue to possess you.

Prayer frees people from the daily routines of life and allows them to enter into a conversation of universality. It can be very useful if its focus is on kindness, gratitude, compassion, and universal connection. When people pray this way, they can see the intrusion of greedy, insecure thinking into their lives. This, in turn, enables them to build a life that's centered on the values they believe in.

LISTENING TO OTHERS

Listening to another person can also be an act that builds self-awareness. I don't mean any kind of listening, but a particular kind of listening. Can you imagine listening to another person without judgment, evaluation, reaction, or letting your mind wander to your own thoughts?

This kind of listening means shutting down your internal commentator who is always describing what's happening. It's probably chattering as you read these lines: "What commentator?" "Who is he to say so and so?" That's what I mean! It means shutting down your automatically triggered repertoire of thinking that distorts and twists the moment from one of possibility to one of fear and hopelessness in all their guises.

Truly listening involves relating to another person not through your internal filter but in a quiet, observant, connected way. By this I mean putting yourself in the other's shoes, just seeing what that's like. Can you do this now? Can you see that your listening muscle is dormant? Each and every daily contact is a time for exercise, for listening, to "wake up" to the moment, for practice.

Let me give you an example of not listening. I recently attended a cocktail party where a young couple named Bob and Judy asked me about the performance anxiety of one of their children, Andrea. They told me that Andrea was a highly gifted musician but her performance anxiety was thwarting her efforts to build a career in the music field. "Can you do anything for her?" they asked. I said that I didn't know, that I wanted to know more about her first. "What does she want from her life? How much does she want it? How is she approaching dealing with her problem? What are her concerns about failing, performing, etc?" I had lots of questions, and no answers. The parents weren't sure either. In fact, they disagreed on several of my questions.

From the conversation I realized that Bob and Judy hadn't spent a lot of time listening to Andrea. In their diligence as parents, they wanted to help her with their advice and knowledge and now wanted me to fix her somehow. Bob and Judy are not "bad" parents. But their desire to understand, to fix, to change keeps them from listening to their child, which is the only place from which they can support her to act. As the cocktail party conversation moved on to other things, I wondered what would happen to Andrea's anxiety if her parents let their ambition for her go for a moment and really listened.

When you speak with another person it is an opportunity to practice awareness. What a gift we are to each other—the gift of listening.

My lifelong career as a physician has been a great privilege. Daily I get to have intimate conversations with patients and practice listening. Here's what happens. When a patient comes in with a complaint, I automatically begin an internal conversation with myself of analysis and diagnosis. I must do this; after all, I'm legally responsible for certain standards of medical practice. But at the same time, I've learned to periodically set aside my automatic thinking—the thinking that lives in my "doctor" structure—and listen to my patient as a fellow human being, as Reynell taught me. The patient is a person, my customer, my responsibility, not just a disease. In this process of connecting we are both enriched, and we dissolve the bonds of aloneness, if even for a fleeting moment. We realize ourselves when we truly listen. Patients thus can become my meditation.

Freed from the filter of my judging mind, I can "hear" my patients' concerns, their fears, and their anxieties. Then, I can respond to them as a person *and* as a doctor, two personas each with a different mission and result. People sense when you're really listening to them, or when you're judging and analyzing. They know it in their bones. Truly listening is another lifelong practice ever available to us. It's a gift that we give to others and to ourselves in the doing.

BODY KNOWLEDGE

Listening to your body is another form of awareness. We easily deceive ourselves with social camouflage, like social infantry soldiers. We make such statements as: "No, I'm not worried" when we're scared to death, or "No, I'm not jealous" when we radiate the green of envy, or "Afraid of intimacy, not me" as we return to our relational or physical isolation. We say these things with a false smile on our faces.

But our bodies tell a different story, if only we would listen. When your mouth is very dry, or you're sweating profusely, what is your body telling you about what's true for you? When your neck is tight and your eyes dry and burning, what is your body telling you about yourself? When you suddenly feel a wave of fatigue or distraction, what is your body saying to you? When, one hour after a meal, you suddenly feel hunger, what is your body saying? Listen! It's all there for the listening.

You have within your grasp at all times an exquisite instrument for discovering, experiencing, and managing "your truth," not "the truth." Your body doesn't lie. On the contrary, it provides a way for living a life of authenticity, reliability, and power—if only you will listen. You can't fool your body—you can intoxicate it, overfeed it, overwork it, but it keeps telling you the truth.

Awareness of your feelings is important, but how you use those feelings is critical. Your feelings are not like radar; they don't tell you the truth about an outside world. They are a reflection of your structure and of your past as manifested in the present. However, and here is the tricky part, your feelings are "true" for you, and you must respect them, as you would respect the feelings of others.

Sometimes you have to ask someone to stop doing something that triggers bad feelings and emotions in you. You need to learn how to do this without blame and with full responsibility and caring for yourself and the other. Blame doesn't work. The alternative is to repress your feelings or walk away from the relationship.

People who care about you care about how you feel. Communicating how you feel to them helps them in relating to you. This is particularly so when you communicate to them in a mood of building and strengthening the relationship, not in a mood of blaming them for how you feel.

Awareness of your body allows you to act with dignity and power. Think of a great artist, a concert performer, or a great teacher. They act in awareness of their bodies, not hiding their anger, frustration, fear, or resignation. Even though we don't fully understand scientifically why authenticity and self-awareness empower us, this fact has been recognized for centuries. Martin Buber, the Jewish philosopher, described this reality clearly:

> What is meant by unification of the soul would be misunderstood if "soul" were taken to mean anything but the whole man, body, mind and spirit together. The soul is not really united unless all bodily energies, all the limbs of the body are united. The Baal-Shem [a major figure in the Hasidic tradition] interpreted the biblical passage "Whatsoever thy hands do, do it with thy might" to mean that the deeds one does should be done with every limb, i.e., even the whole of man's physical being should participate in it, no part should remain outside. A man who thus becomes a unity of body and spirit—he is a man whose work, and life is all of a piece.

Without body awareness, you cut off part of yourself, become less healthy, less effective, and weak. In its extreme, you become dangerous to yourself and others.

Morality and ethics live in your body. This may sound strange to you, but it's so. But when we act badly toward others, when we cheat or steal or kill, when we lie, our body "feels" bad. When we deceive others, ignore their pain, deny our universal connectedness, we feel bad. If we can ignore this bad feeling, we can do anything. We are capable of true cruelty. Think of the recent situation in Kosovo in which people on both sides slaughtered other humans. To do this they had to numb themselves to the evil they're doing with political narratives.

Then they can ignore the fear and anger in their bodies. In this way morality and ethics, as well as health and relationship, require body awareness.

Acceptance

We are only human beings, but we have forgotten that. We learn along the course of our lives many wonderful things, but also develop habits that enable us to survive difficult circumstances in our family, school, work, friendships, careers, etc.

Much of this learning happens outside of our awareness. For example, you may not intend to be a perfectionist, but you learn that perfectionism seems safer in your environment. It's the way to be. Or you may not intend to be arrogant, but the fear that you might not be all-knowing is so great that this "front" is safer for you. And so forth. We learn to do what works for us in the context we live in.

And so it is along the course of your life. Your pure, innocent, childlike nature becomes encrusted with ways that you use to remain safe, loved, successful, happy, etc. We live with historic shards—our "have to be's." They are habits that may have "worked" in the past, but now are barriers to our peace and wellness.

The "have to be" part is what generates suffering and illness. If you "have to be" in control, learning and intimacy are impossible. If you "have to be" right and arrogant, then partnership is impossible. If you "have to be" pessimistic, then innovation and creativity are difficult. Your "have to be's," what some call your ego, keep you from living fully, and also generate your discontent.

Robert, the High Achiever

Robert commented on the "have to be" conversation. "I've lived my life in this 'have to be' way, always needing to be better, to fulfill my family's mission. To be a successful Jewish lawyer, a 'big' lawyer in the community, a credit to my family, that was my 'have to be.' "

He went on: "I've asked what do I want—it's what others wanted me to be. I can see that now, without blaming my family or myself. But what should I do?"

I suggested that "should" implied that there was still something outside of himself that he "had to do."

"How else could you look at this?" I asked. Robert looked confused. I suggested, "Look at it like a gift of truth that you have just given yourself."

"The real question is, what do I want to do?" he said, almost in a whisper.

Some "have to be's" indicate personal values, such as telling the truth, honoring parents, not stealing, or having compassion for all living beings. These you must fight for because they adorn your life with dignity. These are the values, the personal declarations that take courage to live. These are the ones that glorify our lives.

But the destructive "have to be's" are the false survival ones, the ones that if they don't happen make you feel as if you could die, such as "If I don't have enough money I'll die"; "If I don't marry soon I'll die"; "If I don't get this job I'll die." If life goes along and something happens that doesn't look consistent with your "have to be's," you feel helpless—a victim of life. You can enter into despair as you encounter your habitual nature. This has happened to each one of us in our work life, our social life, our families, or in connection with our health.

Falling ill, for example, is for many of us an encounter with a habitual reaction to unwanted events. We think we "have to be" alive and healthy as if it is our right. When we become ill, old reactions come up. We might get angry: "This damn body." Or we might be terrified: "I might die." Or we might feel helpless: "There is nothing anyone can do." Or we might feel out of control: "I should be able to do something." All of these reactions to something not being the way it "has to be" make our illnesses worse.

Moments of awareness, when we see our "system of thought" at work, when we see our habitual reactions, call for noble gentleness toward ourselves. This is the first step in learning compassion. True compassion means recognizing, without judgment, conditioned tendencies in oneself or in another person.

Walter, the Angry Man

Recall that Walter was disturbed by a conversation about anger and the heart. Following this discussion, he began to detect signs of anger in himself and observe them when they appeared. He also began to become an observer of moment-to-moment changes in his body.

Walter told us in class that while driving down the Southeast Expressway in Boston, his anger response was triggered by each car that passed him, or changed lanes, or blew its horn. He understood what "road rage" was about—him.

He said, "I'm just anger waiting to happen, aren't I?"

As he said this, his face beamed with a glow of truth and acceptance that I had never seen in him before. There were tears in his eyes—quiet tears, not tears of rage.

The alternative to acceptance is guilt, blame, anger, self-flagellation, or more "shoulds," another litany of rules. This only deepens our habits of judgment and keeps us frozen. As Bohm indicated, deep "proprioception" without judgment allows the possibility of freedom. In the Tibetan language, *compassion* is translated as "nobility or greatness of heart." This is the meaning of true acceptance. As you awaken and learn, I invite you to bring this orientation to yourself.

Action

Developing awareness and compassion for yourself shifts your world from one of certain suffering to one of new possibilities, of new intimacies, of true healing. It opens the space for new actions.

Taking new actions is important because with recurrence and practice you'll develop an altered structure, a new body, a new mind, and a new set of automatic actions that are more consistent with your current values, with fewer shards from your past.

As you develop an attentive, forgiving awareness of your habitual responses, certain practices will arise and will accelerate your learning. The exercise sections allow you to further embody the distinctions of this book and build new repertoires for action. For this section, I'll outline, in a more general way, some practices that I and others have found useful.

BODY PRACTICES

☐ *Meditation:*   This is useful not only for building awareness, but for restoring body centering and homeostasis (the technical word for physiological balance).

☐ *Yoga:*   This heightens your body awareness and sensibility, as well as providing other benefits like increased mobility and flexibility.

☐ *Breathing practices:*   When you're triggered into an emotional reaction of fear, anger, anxiety, etc., shifting your breathing from fearful shallowness to deep, lung-filling, confident abdominal breaths helps you become quiet and regain your balance.

☐ *Massage and other body disciplines:*   These help you build awareness of learned body tendencies and tensions, as was the case with my mother. The body can be retrained directly by these disciplines. As your body shifts, as you develop in essence a "new" body, so does the unity of your "system of thought." This forms the basis for the work of Rubenfeld, Feldenkrais, Reich, the Lomi school, and others.

SERVICE

Rumi, the Sufi mystic and philosopher, said, "When I don't know who I am, I serve you. When I know who I am, I am you." My understanding of this notion is that when I'm lost or confused and isolate myself and try to figure it out, the dilemma just gets worse. The thoughts mushroom in increasing complexity. If, instead, I find some action of service, or work, or discipline that I consider useful or beneficial and do it, I begin to return to my center.

The service of others requires listening to them, taking actions, and producing satisfaction in them. All of these tend to break oneself out of one's thought prison, and at the same time to confirm one's value.

LEARNING

Guided learning based on awareness can be a lifelong practice for health and growth. In the exercise sections, you've gotten a taste of this kind of learning and have seen how it can serve you. It will help you to design a lifelong program of your own.

Jacob's Ladder

The search for learning has been the work of people throughout the ages. Man has always yearned to reach higher, to gain more understanding and greater peace. The learning in this book is part of that tradition. Moreover, I'm convinced that the search itself, both in my case and in the case of my patients, creates health.

According to Martin Buber, the Hasidic tradition believes that God created the world and then retreated into the heavens. Man's task is to unite the two domains, heaven and earth. Buber wrote: "Man was created for the purpose of unifying the two worlds. He contributes towards this unity by holy living, at the place on which he stands."

Buber goes on to say:

> God's grace consists precisely in this, that He wants to let Himself be won by man, that He places Himself into man's hands. God wants to come to His world, but He wants to come to it through man. But we can let Him in only where we really stand, where we live, where we live a true life.

This may be real for some, metaphoric for others, but a wise goal for all of us who seek health.

As related in the Old Testament, Jacob had a dream about this process in life. A stairway was set on the ground and its top reached to the sky, and angels of God were going up and down it. And God said, "Remember, I will not leave you until I have done what I have promised you."

Denise Levertov, the great American poet, expanded on this image of reaching for God in her poem "Jacob's Ladder."

I share Levertov's view—the ascent is a challenge to your courage and dedication, but through it your life ascends.

We started this journey with the story of a physician frustrated in his task of caring for human suffering. In the journey, I saw that my suffering and the suffering of each of my patients could only be dealt with from "the place on which he stands," as Buber says.

My training enabled me to diagnose and treat disease and pain, but I couldn't empower others or myself to heal. My deepest wish is that you've been inspired to heal yourself, and others.

The exercise sections will allow you to bring what you have begun to learn more deeply into your own life, to achieve peace and wellness for yourself. It's time to create a new mind and build a new body. It's time for you to climb your own Jacob's ladder.

EXERCISES

Major Points in Chapter 6

□ David Bohm invented the notion of "thought as a system." By this he means that your thoughts, perceptions, feelings, emotions, speech, and actions work together as a unity. For example, if you think sad thoughts, you cry, feel "blue," and are unlikely to have a party or participate in any other joyful activity.

He makes three further points:

□ First, thought shows you a world of its making. What you see is a product of your thoughts, not an external reality. If you lived at a time in which the shared thought was that the world was flat, you'd believe the horizon would look like an edge and you could fall off.

□ Second, thought fools you into thinking that you're seeing the world as it is. You forget that you're reacting to a world shaped by your own thoughts.

□ Third, until you perceive thought as the creator of your experience, it controls your life.

Bohm says that you become aware of your thought in the way you sense physical movements and postures—by "proprioception." With the practice of awareness, or proprioception of thought, you can observe your system of thinking, including your actions, mood, thoughts, perceptions, etc.

□ Three fundamental components of change assist you in designing change and learning for yourself: awareness, acceptance, and action, the Three A's of Learning. These elements are not linear; that is, they don't happen in a stepwise fashion. Rather, you can weave them into a pattern of change that works for you. I call this "learning to learn."

□ Using meditation, you can develop the capacity to observe your thinking, your bodily reactions, your emotional predispositions, and your actions as they occur. You've been engaged in this practice throughout the exercise sections. Your meditation is a core practice. Attention is the skill of self-observation. But other practices can reveal your system of thought, including automatic writing, deep listening to another person, taking a quiet but conscious walk, repetitive physical exercise, sitting in solitude in a comfortable chair, or engaging in ritual prayer.

☐ Acceptance involves generating a mood of compassion with which to view yourself and others as you become aware of your and their habitual patterns. Compassion involves lovingly embracing yourself and others. This gives you the ground to stand on for making changes in your life. At this moment in time, the way you are is the result of all that has gone before—how you've been molded by your personal and your species' history. You've learned history's lessons well—you've survived. But what you've learned may not be appropriate for your life as it is now. However, your past capacity for learning shows how well you can learn. Give yourself credit for this and build on this capacity.

☐ Action consists of practices that help you engage in building a new body that will allow you more peace and satisfaction.

These actions include body practices like yoga, breathing exercises, massage, therapeutic approaches like Feldenkrais and Alexander work, the Somatics of Heckler, and, of course, balanced nutrition and exercise.

In addition, actions also involve linguistic practices, like listening to assessments as assessments, declining requests, etc.—the material covered extensively in chapter 4 will build a new observer and a new you. Listening deeply to another is a new practice for lifelong expansion.

Such actions also consist of emotional practices such as observing your emotions, not seeing them as "the truth" but as somatic manifestations of what is true for you at that moment, and acting with others so that you're taken care of and respected.

Life is your most loyal teacher; it keeps showing your system of thought to you. But compassionate, trusted others—family members, good friends, teachers, coaches—can help you build awareness of your patterns by sharing with you their grounded assessments of you. You cannot learn without the eyes of others. Every accomplished and great person has had and continues to have teachers. In this book, I've been your teacher and coach.

☐ The rest is up to you. You need to practice the exercises in the book. At the end of the book, I've provided references to other practices that will heighten your awareness of self, compassion for yourself, and developing new actions. I invite you to continue expanding your awareness and acceptance of yourself. As you do, the new distinctions you've learned will become clearer and more useful. There's no substitute for practice. It's the only way to modify your body and grow in strength and wisdom.

Awareness Exercise

Consider making the awareness exercise a lifelong activity, at least four or five times a week. Build it into your daily schedule for up to twenty minutes a day.

Some people find it helpful to join a meditation group because it helps them if they're immersed with other learners.

Exercises for Reflection and Learning

If you've been reading attentively, you've discovered plenty of distinctions for observation and change. The rest is up to you. You have to begin to live some of the distinctions and invent practices and networks of support that further your learning.

Rather than having you do more exercises, I'll describe the learning programs that my patients invented for themselves. Use what you can when building your own program. Remember, the learning you're doing in this book is for a lifetime.

The shift from resignation to learning is fundamental for health and a rich life. Suffering is the portal of entry into learning. Short-term suffering in this way can be useful; it can motivate. Lifelong suffering is a tragedy and a waste.

Gretchen, the Perfectionist

Gretchen has become aware of her pervasive fear of not being "right." She experiences this in her thoughts, her muscles, and her gut. It has deprived her of a career, of finding someone to share her life with.

Gretchen has begun to view her right-behavior-seeking way of living as rigid and destructive. Sometimes she sees this only the day after it shows itself. But when Gretchen becomes aware of her historic pattern, she stops and changes her behavior. For example, she's making requests of others and is declining some of the requests made of her. Her friends are praising her effort and telling Gretchen how much they like this new woman. Some have said that she has more dignity.

Gretchen still occasionally has a bowel problem, but she now knows that it reflects her orientation toward life at that moment. She is no longer phobic about cancer and visits her doctor only for annual check-ups. She uses her bowel "signals" to look at where in her life she's afraid or anxious—where she's gripped by the fearful voice of her mother.

Gretchen has taken other actions as well. She has begun a yoga class at a local church. She finds that this relaxes not only her body, but her thoughts. Her instructor commented in the opening session about how stiffly Gretchen held her body. This problem and her emotional rigidity were a single unified phenomenon. She has also joined a local health club, where she hopes to meet new friends and possible suitors.

Gretchen meditates every day and refers to the course notes and exercises often. To increase her self-knowledge, she has enrolled in an autobiography writing workshop at a local university. But the most amazing thing Gretchen has done is to join an African dance class. "It's wild and crazy. It's very hard for me; I never let myself be that way before, but it's fun," she said.

Walter, the Angry Man

Walter now laughs on occasion, and sometimes even at himself.

He still falls into anger, but he can see its early warning signals. Walter has learned to take deep breaths when he feels himself being seized by his old demon. Most of the time he can tame it, but not always. Walter has stopped beating himself up when he realizes that he's lost it again. "I'm only a beginner," he told me.

Walter has taken actions to help his heart problem. Since finishing the course, Walter has cut his smoking by 80 percent and wants to quit completely. He has joined a gym and works out three times a week. And he's eating healthier foods.

Walter's learning has generated both compassion for himself and for others. Since he realized that he had poor early teachers in the art of living, he joined the Big Brother organization to, as he says, "help someone else escape from the pain that I've had." He's a Big Brother to a twelve-year-old African-American boy named Antoine. Walter told me recently, "Antoine is just like I was, angry and distrustful. We're becoming buddies. Just think," he went on, "I never said anything good about a black person before!"

Robert, the High Achiever

Robert made a major change in his life when he saw how driven he was and how the message "You must be successful" was destroying his health and peace of mind. He realized that his ambitions were not of his own making but were those of his family. Robert was tired of not doing work that he liked. He requested and got a year's leave of absence from his law firm.

Robert found a job as a writing coach at a local boy's school. He loved being with the young students, helping them to learn for the sake of learning. Robert likes teaching so much he's toying with the idea of going back to school for his education degree. He says, "It really turns me on. I'm very interested in how people learn."

Robert is also taking a tai chi class, which he finds fascinating and relaxing. "It's so un-Jewish," he says.

Now that he's taken these steps, he and his wife are eagerly awaiting the birth of their first child.

Linda, the Depressed Woman

After the course was over, Linda began seeing a psychiatrist. She had heard of antidepressants and wanted to use them to "get on her feet." The therapist agreed and prescribed one. It helped Linda tremendously, and her depression lifted.

As she began to feel better, Linda asked herself how she would like to use her life. Although she had always wanted to be a schoolteacher, Linda didn't think it was a practical option at her age. Instead, she began to sell some of her needlework and knitting at local craft shows. Then Linda had the idea that she could teach others about what she knew. It worked. She's teaching a course at a local adult education center. The class starts in about a month as I write this. Already five people have enrolled. "One of them is a man. Can you imagine that?" she said to me.

Things have also improved in Linda's personal life. After many years of not vacationing together, she and her family rented a cabin in the New Hampshire woods. She says, "We've been alone for so long together. I'm a little afraid, but it'll be good." The "ghost" of her own inadequacy is disappearing. Finally, after all these years, Linda senses she can shape her own life.

Post-test

Remember the test you took in chapter 1? I'd like you to take it again now. Compare your results from each test. Do you notice any differences? How do you feel about them? Do they help strengthen your commitment to lifelong learning?

I. Self-efficacy.

This behavioral characterization reflects two dimensions of human existence: the presence of ambition, and the sense that one can make the changes necessary to achieve that ambition. Together they allow a person to pursue meaningful goals. Self-efficacy and meaning are major health enhancers; their absence is a health risk.

Typical Profile of Each Quadrant

1. **Learner:** You make personal declarations and back them up with learning and change. You achieve success and may lead others.
2. **Frustrated:** You have lofty visions but can't mobilize to fulfill them. Frustration is common.
3. **Pedant:** Learners without ambition "stockpile" information and are often boring and pedantic.
4. **Resigned:** You are without ambition, and change is difficult. Life looks bleak and repetitive.

II. Social Ease.

I have combined two dimensions in this way of looking at human behavior. The first is trust: Are you able to enter into trusting relationships, even intimate ones? Second, are you able to retain autonomy and dignity in linguistic interactions with others: to decline gracefully, to listen to the assessments of others constructively, and to make requests when necessary? These two dimensions taken together define what I call social ease, and represent a major health enhancer or risk factor.

Self-efficacy (a "Can-Do" Attitude)

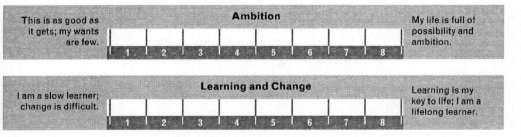

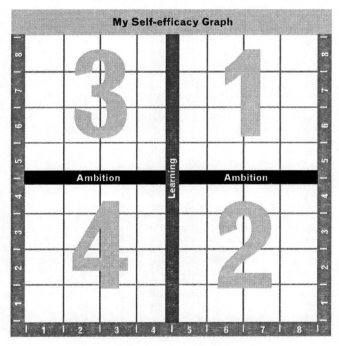

Typical Profile of Each Quadrant

1. **Effective partner:** You trust and enter relationships and intimacy, but keep your sense of self intact.
2. **Dependent:** You cling to others for meaning and direction.
3. **Lone Ranger:** You are independent and unattached, the American ideal.
4. **Isolated:** You distrust others and avoid intimacy. Eventually you isolate yourself.

Social Ease (Comfort and Intimacy with Others)

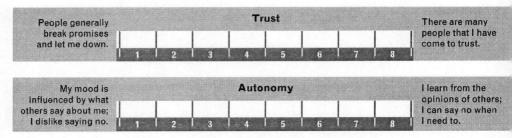

| People generally break promises and let me down. | **Trust** | | | | | | | | There are many people that I have come to trust. |
| My mood is influenced by what others say about me; I dislike saying no. | **Autonomy** | | | | | | | | I learn from the opinions of others; I can say no when I need to. |

III. Emotional Skills.

This set of behavioral skills has recently been described by Daniel Goleman. Emotional intelligence (EI) appears to be important for success and health.

Emotional Skills (Dealing with Feelings)

I don't generally notice my feelings; I am a practical person.	Emotional Awareness 1 2 3 4 5 6 7 8	I generally notice my feelings and those of others.
When I have bad feelings I try to ignore them or distract myself.	Open Communication 1 2 3 4 5 6 7 8	I openly share my feelings and use them to help build relationships.

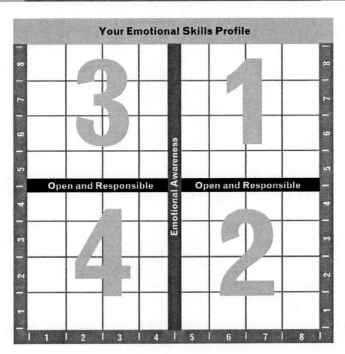

Your Emotional Skills Profile

In general, there are two aspects of emotional intelligence. First, people with high EI are aware of their feelings moment by moment. They honor, respect, and are aware of their own emotional life and that of others. Second, they take care of their emotional lives. When they are in discomfort they make that known to others in a nonblaming but behavior-changing way. Additionally, they attend to the discomfort of others.

Typical Profile of Each Quadrant

1. **Emotional intelligence:** Good partners, team players, leaders.
2. **Emotional "bull in china shop":** Open, but very little awareness of emotional life of self or others. Unaware of reaction of others to his/her expressiveness.
3. **Silent Sufferer:** Feels social pain, but "stuck" with it.
4. **Alexithymia:** Unaware of own feelings, closed to feelings of others. People in this category are disconnected from intimate relationships and often are mechanical in their behavior.

Commencement

For many years I found it odd that the end of a school year or graduation from college was called *commencement*. In the context of this book, I understand better how an ending can also be a beginning. In the course of reading the chapters and doing the exercises, you've been learning new distinctions, much as I did when I went to medical school.

Like most things of value, these distinctions seem simple, almost self-evident. Living these distinctions is another matter.

You've seen that first and foremost *people are animals* and as such are governed by biological laws. Your behaviors are determined by your structure, genetically given and historically molded. You are a machine that can learn.

You've also seen that *you exist as a whole entity,* not as the sum of your parts. When you're angry, your heart is involved as much as your thoughts. When you're depressed, your immune system is involved as much as your mood.

You've also discovered that *you are a special kind of animal—one that lives in "a house of language."* Your use of language is intimately connected with your history, culture, mood, sense of self, picture of the future, and especially in how you live in social situations with others.

Finally, you have seen that *you have the capacity for self-awareness.* This state is not easily available, but it is attainable through practice, with the help of others and a commitment to telling the truth. The expression "The truth will set you free" describes a shift from a historically determined certainty to a realm of possibility and creativity.

This search for the truth involves two realities—freedom is possible, learning is never over. Once you free yourself from one bardo (the place that you're stuck in at the moment), another will appear. But each time you let go into the moment just as it is, you'll become stronger and freer. You ascend a rung in Jacob's ladder. You'll have a moment of new beginning and experience well-being.

A Time of "Jumping Together"

Life has no accidents. The forces of life are so huge we can only glimpse them. Whatever your spiritual orientation, you must see how very tiny we are on the cosmic stage. Yet, even at the same moment that you see that, you must also see that we alone among the animals are unique—we can act out of biological and historical mechanisms, but we can also create. Our task in living in the world of the new millennium, changing as it is with blinding speed, is to continually rebuild ourselves so that we can generate lives of peace, caring, loving, community, family—all of the things that we value even as the world whirls around us.

For centuries, man has reached to know and understand himself in search of a better life. The great scientists, philosophers, religious leaders, psychologists, and healers of the East and West have sought, each within his or her own culture and discipline, timeless answers. In the West, the major mode of validation of truth over the past two centuries has been rational and reductionistic. Proof has been through logic, showing how parts generate larger phenomena.

Proof has not always been sought in this way alone. In the fifteenth century, for example, there was another method of validation. When observers from different points of view, say a scientist and a philosopher, arrived at the same set of insights, that was taken as a kind of proof. The name given to this form of proof is *consilience,* literally a "jumping together."

This book represents consilience thinking. I offer a tapestry, largely woven for me by my teachers, pulling together threads from the East, the West, from biology, philosophy, linguistics, and psychology into a consilience learning program for you.

In the new millennium, my suspicion is that some of our most powerful thinking will be consilience thinking. As we deal with ethnic resentment, environmental pollution, information overload, and an aging population, in a context in which, despite the fact that more and more people are well fed and living in democracies, there is not abundant joy and peace, we need a new approach to our problems. I think that consilience thinking could inform us as we look at our larger problems.

What does spirituality have to say about health, about crime, about pollution? What does biology have to say about learning, about diversity, about our companies and productivity? What does language study have to offer to health professionals, to leaders, to teachers? What does somatic wisdom offer us as we seek health and effectiveness? These are consilience questions for the next years.

After having spent a whole book questioning you and assigning tasks to you, I make one final request. I invite you to use this book as a commencement moment in your life. Like any commencement, sadness mingles with possibility. The sadness is about the end of schooling, of being taught and led, of being in a sense dependent. The possibility is generated by having glimpsed the future—one of wellness, peace, love, and compassion, combined with courage and passion.

Woody Guthrie used to end his concerts with the following phrase: "Take it easy, but take it."

Readings

This is a representative selection of books that were critical to me in my learning. I provide this list and a brief description of each one as a resource for those who want to know more about the theoretical basis of this book. Remember, however, that knowing more and living life in the light of what you know are two different states. Walking the talk is different from talking the talk so don't be fooled.

Boss, Medard, *The Existential Foundations of Medicine and Psychology* (Holmes, PA: Jason Aronson, 1979, 1983).
> This is a pioneering thought piece on mind-body relationships. Medard Boss was a Swiss psychiatrist who actually was Martin Heidegger's therapist. During his long acquaintance with Heidegger, Boss was deeply influenced by his philosophy and wove it into a new, though cumbersome, holistic psychiatry. This is a brilliant, pioneering work, worthy of the effort required to read it.

Bohm, David, *Thought as a System* (New York: Routledge, 1992).
> David Bohm is a renowned quantum physicist and philosopher. In this book he proposes that we act as a coordinated system of thinking, feeling, acting, and perceiving and that this system generates our experience. He also proposes "proprioception" of thought, an awareness of the movement of thought that allows change. His work is consistent with modern scientific views of the working of the brain.

Capra, Fritjof, *The Web of Life: A New Scientific Understanding of Living Systems* (New York: Anchor Books, 1996).
> Capra synthesizes the work of Maturana, Varela, and Flores to develop an ecologically positioned understanding of cognition and linguistic coordination in communities. Capra talks about how the traditional reductionist way of thinking "has alienated us from nature, and from our fellow human beings. To regain our full humanity we have to regain our experience of connectedness with the whole web of life."

Cole, Michael, *Cultural Psychology: A Once and Future Discipline* (Cambridge, MA: Belknap Harvard Press, 1996).
In this book Cole shows "Culture as the special medium of human life. Mediation through culture is the special characteristic of human thought and this perspective fits with current ideas in cognitive science, developmental psychology, and anthropology."

Edelman, Gerald M., *Bright Air, Brilliant Fire: On the Matter of the Mind* (New York: Basic Books, 1992).
This is the third in a trilogy of books, the others being *Neural Darwinism* and the *Remembered Present,* in which the author proposes a biologically based theory of cognition and learning that is at once scientifically sound and, at the same time, central for the emerging holistic view as discussed by Capra, Flores, Goleman, Bohm, and others.
This book presents a biologic description of cognition and action that is totally consistent with the holistic principles of this book.

————, "Building a Picture of the Brain," *Daedalus,* Spring 1998.
A shorter presentation of Edelman's provocative thinking and research.

Goleman, Daniel, *Emotional Intelligence* (New York: Bantam Books, 1995).
Goleman begins to distinguish a form of intelligence that appears to be unique—emotional intelligence. It involves body awareness of the self and others, and the ability to take effective social action informed by the body's state. I am certain, and our preliminary studies confirm, that lack of this awareness is a health risk factor.

Hanh, Thich Nhat, *The Miracle of Mindfulness* (Boston: Beacon Press, 1975); Beck, Charlotte Joko, *Everyday Zen: Love and Work* (San Francisco: Harper & Row, 1989).
These two books were very useful to me as I began a meditation practice. The first book, by the Vietnamese Zen master Thich Nhat Hanh, includes procedural instructions and encouragement to the beginner. The second book gives useful coaching for the beginner in meditation, along with some key elements to watch for as your practice develops. There are many other books on meditation, the relaxation response, and awareness. These provide a beginning orientation to the Buddhist way of describing meditation. Descriptions of similar experiences can be found in most of the world's major religions. But in Buddhism, meditation is a core practice, hence I present these references.

Harrington, Anne, *The Placebo Effect: An Interdisciplinary Exploration* (Cambridge, MA: Harvard University Press, 1997).

The placebo effect places languaging, expectation, and physiologic change in close relation. Several experts describe this effect and some of the classic interpretations of it. The placebo effect is one of a class of healing traditions through human interaction in language. Included are spiritual healing, hypnosis, and mesmerism.

Heckler, Richard Strozzi, *The Anatomy of Change: A Way to Move Through Life's Transitions* (Berkeley, CA: North Atlantic Books, 1993).

Heckler is my teacher in applied somatic learning. The shards of our past are also held in our body as "conditioned tendencies" or armoring. Direct attention to these phenomena and the intention for learning directed to these somatic tendencies can shift the being—the system of thought.

Heckler is an aikido master, a brilliant teacher and writer, and a consilience thinker whose insights in this and his other books are well worth listening to.

————, *Holding the Center: Sanctuary in a Time of Confusion* (Emeryville, CA: Frog, Ltd., 1997).

Beautifully presented background distinctions of observing the life of the body. Heckler's books provide rich distinctions for observing action in the moments of living. Observing in real time, and building new practices for change on a foundation of self-acceptance and compassion.

LeDoux, Joseph, *The Emotional Brain: The Mysterious Underpinnings of Emotional Life* (New York: Simon & Schuster, 1996).

Our emotions also have a biologic basis, and, like all biologic phenomena, they are structure determined and subject to "learning," both historic and intentional. This book demonstrates these phenomena in a reader-friendly way.

Maturana, Humberto R., and Varela, Francisco J., *The Tree of Knowledge: The Biological Roots of Human Understanding* (Boston, MA: New Science Library, 1987).

In this most amazing book, Maturana and Varela show how, on biologic grounds alone, the Cartesian hypothesis is flawed. They indicate how the aspects of human life might arise from biologic processes alone. They also describe the biologic basis of language.

Winograd, Terry, and Flores, Fernando, *Understanding Computers and Cognition: A New Foundation for Design* (Reading, MA: Addison-Wesley, 1995).
  This book is a Trojan horse—a radically new view of human nature and communication is enunciated in a book that puts computers into a human context. In the first six chapters, the authors put forth a synthesis of traditions that brings light to the areas of human cognition, communication, and language. They do this as a prelude to building an understanding of computers. The first chapters stand on their own and have been central to my understanding.

Index

ABOUT THE AUTHORS

MATTHEW BUDD, M.D., former assistant professor at Harvard Medical School, was the architect of the first behavioral medicine department at the Harvard Community Health Plan and developer of the revolutionary "Ways to Wellness" program. His work has been featured on National Public Radio and in *The New York Times, The Wall Street Journal,* and other national venues. He lives in Boston, Massachusetts. LARRY ROTHSTEIN, Ed.D., is a leading collaborator on self-help books, including Joan Borysenko's *Minding the Body, Mending the Mind.* He lives in Boston.